MAX & ME

The Abuse of Power in Florida Community Colleges

A Case Study

Marion Brady

Other books by the author:

A Primer for Social Studies (State of Florida)
Idea and Action in American History (Prentice-Hall)
Idea and Action in World Cultures (Prentice-Hall)
What's Worth Teaching? Selecting, Organizing and Integrating Knowledge (State University of New York Press)
A Study of Reality (Books for Educators)

Publisher
Marion Brady
4285 N. Indian River Drive
Cocoa, Florida 32927

It rains upon the just,
And on the unjust fella;
But mostly on the just, because
Unjust has Just's umbrella.

— Adapted

Unheeded advice from my wife:

"Never try to teach a pig to sing.
It wastes your time and annoys the pig."

Dedicated to the victims.

CONTENTS

FOREWORD

Marion Brady, the "me" of *Max & Me*, is both my friend and my former colleague at Brevard Community College. As my friend I know him to be an articulate, intelligent, and brave man. If he has a flaw—if it can be called a flaw—it is his reluctance to accept discretion as the better part of valor, his refusal to give it up and walk away, his unwillingness to shrug and turn his back on what he sees as corruption, injustice, and stupidity. If he were not a man of such principles, he would still be teaching at BCC.

As an educator, Brady's record speaks for itself—his national and international recognition, his role as consultant to both public and private education organizations, his numerous books and articles, his 25 years as a Brevard County educator, the testimony of his former students—and it gives him a stature far above the average of BCC faculty. As an educator he has been a credit to himself and to the college.

And then in the spring of 1992, BCC President Maxwell C. King petitioned the Board of Trustees to fire Marion Brady. As a result of that petition and other administrative actions by King, in August 1992 Brady and others (with the backing of the United Faculty of Florida) filed suit against King and the Board of Trustees before the U.S. District Court in Orlando. Nevertheless, the college proceeded with its own prosecution: the formal "Brady Hearings" on the Cocoa campus of BCC were held during September through December of 1992; the BCC Board of Trustees, even though named in the federal suit in Orlando, sat as both judge and jury. Needless to say, Brady lost; he was officially terminated in March of 1993 after almost a year of "house arrest."

On February 7, 1994, the suit against King and the Board in the district court in Orlando was dismissed, without a hearing, by U.S. District Judge Richard Kellem. Judge Kellem, an 85-year-old visiting judge who never graduated from college or law school, came down from up North for a few weeks of the winter in Florida and dismissed Brady's suit one week before it was scheduled to be heard.

Then on March 4, 1994, the suit was joined by the National Education Association (NEA), representing literally millions of teachers across America, and an appeal of Judge Kellem's decision was filed before the 11th U.S. Circuit Court of Appeals in Atlanta, where it currently awaits review.

Max & Me is Professor Brady's account of his experiences with the Florida Community College System in general and Brevard Community College in particular. It is largely a difficult and complicated story about life as an instructor at BCC. Brady's allegations against Maxwell C. King, his power and role as president of BCC, and against King's subordinates such as Robert Aitken (Provost of the Melbourne campus) and Stevan McCrory (former Dean of Liberal Arts and Business on the Melbourne campus) will not come as a shock to anyone familiar with Florida's community colleges.

During the original "Brady Hearings" before the Board of Trustees in the fall of 1992, many faculty and administrators were called to testify. I received a formal subpoena along with eight or ten of my colleagues on the Melbourne campus, and we all testified under oath to what had happened. Many others were willing and would have testified as well, but the trustees finally denied further witnesses to the same effect, saying they understood and accepted our testimony. King and his administration, however, denied the faculty's account of events, saying we "misunderstood" and were "misinformed," claiming essentially that we were lying under oath, perjuring ourselves before the board.

The net result of the hearings, in short, was to pit the administration of the college against the very teachers it is designed to support. Ideally, a college administration is supposed to make the institution run smoothly, to facilitate the educational process, to enable teachers to do what they do best, teach. At BCC, and too many other community colleges in Florida, the faculty have been made the enemy.

At the very least, one hopes that *Max & Me* will crack open the door to public awareness and scrutiny of Florida's community colleges in general and BCC in particular. Readers of the book will come to see that Professor Brady's concern is not "getting his job back," as *Florida Today* suggests, or personal revenge against Max King for firing him. Brady's goal is simply and clearly the reform of a system he sees as unjust, a system he describes as out of control and without checks and balances, a system which, he argues, desperately needs public input and oversight.

I wish him well.

Jeff Neill
Department of English
Melbourne Campus, BCC

AUTHOR'S NOTE

I've gone to considerable lengths to assure the accuracy of *Max & Me*. Most of the story was drawn directly from documents produced during or immediately after the described events. When others provided me with information, I gave them pre-publication photocopies of the manuscript, asked them to check it for accuracy, and sign their names when my account squared with their memories.

I have 31 such documents on file, from all excepting a few hostile College administrators.

MAX & ME

Part I

DEAR JUDGE:

Your Honor, I'm not sure you understand the situation. We're talking plain, old-fashioned corruption. And, unless something's done, it's going to get worse.
Maybe a little background information would help put the matter in perspective.
Florida used to have two education providers. At the bottom end of the educational ladder were public schools for students from kindergarten through the 12th grade. They were organized by counties—67 systems, each with a superintendent who answered to an elected school board.
At the top end of the ladder were Florida's publicly supported universities. Each had a president who answered to Florida's Board of Regents.
In the 1950's and 1960's, the community college movement took off nationwide. Florida's legislature joined the movement, eventually creating 28 community colleges.
Originally, these new institutions were just extensions of the existing K-12 county systems. Community college presidents were basically "principals" of schools offering grades 13 and 14. This, of course, meant that community college presidents, like the principals, were under the authority of county superintendents and elected county school boards.
As you can imagine, the arrangement wasn't very popular with most community college presidents. They got together, petitioned the legislature, and got themselves out from under the school boards. Each community college was given a board of trustees appointed by the governor.

That's when the problems began. According to Florida
TaxWatch, the new system of community college governance created a power vacuum. The community college
presidents moved into the vacuum with a vengeance.
It's accepted wisdom that human institutions need
systems of checks and balances to function well. Community college boards of trustees don't check and balance. In
a December 1993 news release, Florida TaxWatch said
that "Community college presidents probably have more
independence and power than any other educators in the
state of Florida. They respond to and affect the perceptions of an appointed board of lay persons who operate
without independent staff in the oversight of multimil-
lion dollar operations that deal with complex and technical issues."

At the K-12 end of Florida's educational system, the
election process motivates candidates to dig out dirt and
hold it up to public scrutiny. All else being equal, the
best dirt digger wins the election. It's messy, but most of
the time it works.

At the university end of Florida's educational system,
there's the Board of Regents, a high-profile bureaucracy.
Potential dirt diggers on this end of the educational spec-
trum include the legislature, the governor, faculty sen-
ates, faculty unions, and the state's newspapers, television and other media. It's less democratic, but with all
those people watching, the most obvious abuses of power
generally come to light.

At the community college level, however, there are all
sorts of built-in pressures to cover dirt up. TaxWatch says
that the 28 individual community college boards have
more powers than the Board of Regents, and a sharp community college president can figure out any number of
ways to channel that power to the mutual advantage of
both administrators and trustees. (Hey, Mr./Ms. Trustee.
How would you like your name on a building? A contract

to supply the College's office furniture? Some inside information on construction bids?)

To compound the problem, most trustees are political campaign contributors. They're usually well off, and are likely to perceive their trustee role in old-fashioned labor-management terms. Seeing themselves less as trustees than as members of a corporate board of directors, they ally themselves with the college's president rather than with the college's students. (Teachers refusing to knuckle under? Fire 'em.)

Your Honor, a survey of the state's newspapers would give you an idea of what kinds of things some of Florida's community college "educational leaders" have done. They've paid themselves outrageous salaries—far higher than the national average. They've surrounded themselves with massive, expensive administrative structures—again, far larger than the national average, which is itself too high. They've fed their egos by naming buildings and even entire campuses after themselves. They've traveled all over the world at taxpayer expense. They've built and maintained private properties using college materials and employees. They've put the catering bill for large, private social functions on the public's tab. They've cut themselves in on lucrative real estate deals. They've used public monies to buy themselves season box seats at expensive sporting events. They've behaved irresponsibly (and even unlawfully) and then stuck the taxpayers for the resulting, often mind-boggling legal bills. And, to silence the whistleblowers who've tried to alert the public to what's going on, they've operated kangaroo courts that make a mockery of due process.

Farmers say, "If you see one rat in the barn, you've probably got a hundred." For every story about betrayal of the public's trust that reporters dig up, you can bet that many more go unreported. (In fact, given the way the system works, the worst abuses are unlikely ever to see the light of day. That's because the really powerful

community college presidents hand-pick their trustees,
and those they pick usually have enough clout to assure
that the local press sees, hears and speaks no evil about
them.)

How much does this sort of thing cost? In dollars,
plenty. In loss of educational quality and respect for educators and education, the costs are incalculable. What are
students learning when they read in their local papers
about administrators and trustees erecting buildings with
public monies and immediately naming them after themselves? When it's discovered that administrators are
engaging in shady business deals? When critics are
framed or unmercifully hounded? When friends and family regularly appear on payrolls or as "consultants"?
When every trustee vote is unanimous? When tight budgets affect everything but administrator perks? When
"justice" is a farce?

Florida's legislature is years late in addressing the
problem of out-of-control community college administrators. The good-ole-boy territory between the K-12 system
and the universities must be fenced in and some rules
laid down. The present situation is intolerable.

Am I stirring a tempest in a teapot? Civilization is
hardly going to rise or fall as a consequence of events
and conditions in Florida's community college system.
However, at the very least, what happens here is part of
the larger picture of education in America. H.G. Wells
once wrote, "Human history becomes, more and more, a
race between education and catastrophe." I think it's fair
to say that, nationwide, in the race between education
and catastrophe, catastrophe is winning. Failure to act in
our own communities and state, where individual effort
can make a great and immediate difference, nods approv-
al of the way the race is going.

Your Honor, I'm going to be telling you mostly about
my experiences at Brevard Community College. You may
wonder if it's fair to generalize about an entire communi-

ty college system from experience in just one. I think it is. I've looked through the files of 21 of the state's newspapers, and listened to scores of employee horror stories. Brevard may not be typical, but it certainly isn't singular. If the abuse and misuse of power I've seen at Brevard can continue for a quarter of a century without hindrance, TaxWatch must be right. There's something fundamentally wrong with the way the whole system is organized.

Old wrongs can't be righted. I'm looking ahead, to what might be done about the continuing **potential** for abuses of power by Florida community college administrations. Even if I lose my own fight for justice and fairness, if it somehow prompts a heightened public awareness of the problem and a determination to do something about it, I'll be content.

DUE PROCESS? YOU'RE JOKING!

I was embarrassed, angry . . . and suspicious.

On Monday, the 7th of February, 1994, Federal Judge Richard Kellem dismissed my suit against the administration of Brevard Community College. Kellem, a visiting judge in the United States District Court for the Middle District of Florida, Orlando Division, said there was no evidence that the board had acted improperly in firing me. He also said the suit was based on suspicion of wrongdoing—not proof.

A reporter from *Florida Today* asked me how I felt.

I told him I was embarrassed—that it would now seem to the general public that we didn't have a case, or that my lawyers didn't know what they were doing, which was certainly not true.

I knew what I knew about Brevard Community College from 16 years as a member of the faculty. I knew also what our witnesses said they were willing to say under oath about the operation of the College: bid-rigging, kickbacks, skimming, nepotism, cronyism, fund diversion—corruption—kept from the public by orchestrated intimidation.

I was also mystified. There were too many unanswered questions. Linda Parrish, president of the Brevard Community College chapter of the United Faculty of Florida, had called me just after the January 1994 meeting of the College's Board of Trustees. A strange little exchange had taken place at the board meeting, she said. With a potential multi-million dollar suit against the administration already on the federal court docket and just three weeks away, Board Attorney Joe Matheny had said that he had nothing to report when the "Legal Actions" item came up on the agenda. Questioned about the case by Trustee Patrick Healy, Matheny hemmed, hawed and finally said nothing substantive.

There was more. In preparation for the trial, my lawyers had sent out dozens of subpoenas. As far as the faculty could determine, Jesse Hogg, the BCC administration's Coral Gables lawyer, had not subpoenaed anyone. Did he know something we didn't know?

And still more. The judge said that I should have appealed the decision to terminate me to the Fifth District Court of Appeals in Daytona Beach—a state court—rather than filing a federal action for alleged violations of the federal constitution. Although going through Florida's courts was an option, my lawyers very deliberately rejected it. Brevard Community College President Maxwell King had, after all, once boasted to several women on the faculty that his connections made him invulnerable. There was also an assumption that the federal system might be slightly less prone than the state courts to reflect the traditional Southern pro-management, anti-union bias.

Finally, and most mystifying of all, we hadn't been approached about settling out of court. We knew that the

administration had seen our witness list. We knew that
they knew that ex-Deans of the College Ann Thomas,
Jasper Trigg, Paul Rehberg, Curt Lezanic and Joanne
Nicholson were on it. All were ex-administrators at BCC,
and each knew enough to shoot holes in the administration's defense. They knew that we intended to call to the
stand ex-security guards at the College—people who
claimed to have first-hand knowledge of felonious activity
engaged in by administrators. They knew that, for every
administrator they could produce to testify about relevant aspects of the case, we could produce a dozen faculty
members who would testify that administrators had, during the course of the hearing that led to my firing, either
perjured themselves or conveniently "forgotten" important facts.

There was also little doubt that the administration
knew we intended to call retired Director of College Food
Services Russ Jones to the stand. Jones had once written
a three-page, single-spaced letter alleging administrative
kickbacks and College funding of construction and maintenance work on two of BCC President Maxwell King's
private properties, and extensive private use of College
materials and labor by Vice President for Maintenance
Harold Creel.

Along with much else, Jones said in his letter:

I catered King's personal and social events for
several years. Many of these affairs were held at
King's ranch in Volusia County. The cost of these
affairs was charged to the cafeteria account, but
I was instructed to submit invoices without price
figures so that [Vice President for Business Af-
fairs] Megregian and [President] King could determine the amount to be credited to the College
cafeteria account. On one occasion, I provided food
and booze for a family reunion in Volusia. All

supplies were transported in College vehicles and
the food was charged to the College cafeteria account. And, as in all other incidents, the amount
credited to this account was determined by Megregian and King. This was a family event.
The last year I managed the cafeteria, I served
approximately 500 people for one of King's social
events. The cost of the affair—charged to College
expense—was well over $3,000. The cafeteria ac-
count was credited with $400. This amount did
not even cover the booze bill which was over $500.

(Exhibit #35*)

Jones concluded his letter with an offer. If there was
doubt about whether or not he was telling the truth, he'd
personally pay the cost of polygraph tests for himself and
certain administrators of his choosing.
Jones was sure the administration had seen the letter
because, he said, King's sidekick, Leon Stearns, had
three times come to Tennessee in an apparent attempt to
talk to him.
This kind of thing added up to potential personal,
political and professional devastation for King and the
BCC administration, yet no effort was made to explore
the possibility of keeping it quiet by settling out of court.

---

* Unless otherwise indicated, all subsequent "Exhibit" citations refer to
the Plaintiffs' Exhibit List, Case No. 92-709-CIV-ORL-18, United States
District Court, Middle District of Florida, Orlando Division: Alan Thornquest, Marion Brady and Thomas Ward, Plaintiffs, vs. Maxwell King,
Robert E. Lawton, Tace T. Crouse, Everett P. Whitehead, Stevan McCrory,
individually and in their official capacities as Administrative Employees
at Brevard Community College; Patrick Healy, John Henry Jones,
Rachael Moehle, Bernard Simpkins and Frank E. Williams, individually
and in their official capacities as Members of District Board of Trustees
of Brevard Community College, Defendant.

What could I conclude? Perhaps there were reasonable explanations for Matheny's board meeting behavior, for the defendants' attorneys not issuing subpoenas, for the judge's insistence that we had made a procedural error, for Jesse Hogg's feeling no need to attempt an out-of-court settlement. However, if there were such explanations, they eluded me.

Unfortunately, from my perspective, the suit wasn't about corruption at BCC; it was about the faculty's right to speak and write publicly about perceived corruption. The legal brief phrased it much more elaborately, of course, but that was the bottom line.

There were three plaintiffs in the suit. Alan Thornquest, long-time BCC counselor, Tom Ward, a full-time sociology teacher, and I were suing the College's president, a few selected administrators, and the trustees, for violating our rights under the First, Fifth and Fourteenth Amendments to the United States Constitution.

Alan was membership chairman of the faculty union, an aggressive organizer and a long-time critic of King's union-busting tactics. In "reorganizing" him out of a job, King had decimated the College's counseling department. Alan had so much seniority that, in order to get to him, almost every other counselor had to be let go. In 1980, when the College had fewer than 10,000 students, there were 13 counselors. In 1993, with more than 15,000 students, only two were left.

Tom Ward was also an active member of the union, but his greater mistakes were two. First, he happened to teach the same subject I taught. Since one of the several strategies the administration was using in attempting to dump me was to eliminate sociology from the curriculum, Tom, as a teacher of sociology with much less seniority, had to go. Tom's second mistake, he was certain, was in crossing Tace Crouse, a fresh new female administrator who, under King, had moved from a local high school mathematics teacher to provost of BCC's Cocoa campus with breathtaking speed.

My own fate seemed to have been primarily a consequence of my asking questions about College contracts, bid procedures, and other matters that I felt needed a public airing. I hadn't set out on a reformist course, but the more questions I asked, the more other BCC employees fed me information about problems. The more information they fed me, the more questions I asked.

Judge Kellem's action dismissing all charges was beyond my comprehension. The trustees, he said, had already given me a fair trial. Never mind the fact that, long before that "trial" began, I had sued my judge and jury—the trustees. How could they come to my case as neutral and unbiased hearers when I had a suit pending against them? Letting me off would say that they thought I was right and almost certainly cause them to lose their case.

Never mind also that the trustees themselves were called as material witnesses. We wanted to know if King or other administrators had ever said anything negative about me to the trustees. To be a legitimate jury, the trustees needed to say "no" under oath. They refused to take the stand.

The judge's opinion was startling, but after 15 years of banging my head against the power structure, I wasn't particularly surprised.

Deprived of the opportunity to tell my story in court, writing it down seemed the healthy thing to do. Even if I never published it, I'd probably feel better. Then too, there was a precedent for locally written descriptions of local abuses of power. Glenda Busick had just published her book, *Brevard's Good Ole Boys*. I knew most Brevardians were more interested in county government than in Brevard Community College, but the reception her book received seemed to indicate that at least some of Brevard's citizens were hungry for information beyond the usual media fare. I began pulling material together and writing.

Max & Me reflected my perspective on the events and conditions at Brevard Community College over the last few years. Stories sharing the same elements could be written by many other faculty at Brevard, Palm Beach, Lake City, Hillsborough, and perhaps other Florida community colleges.

A LITTLE BACKGROUND

I came to Brevard County with 15 years of professional experience in Ohio and Florida secondary schools and colleges. The five years prior to my moving to Brevard County I taught at Florida State University's on-campus demonstration school, and in FSU's Arts and Sciences department. I was hired as Coordinator for Social Studies for Brevard County Schools in 1967, just before Dr. B. Frank Brown was appointed superintendent of Brevard's schools.

Not long after my arrival, a reorganization split the county into three geographic areas. The subject-matter supervisory positions were abolished, and most of my peers moved to administrative positions in other counties or to Florida's Department of Education in Tallahassee. I was asked to stay on as Director of Instruction for Brevard's North Area schools.

A few months into the job I became convinced that the Area Superintendents' offices in general, and my middle-level management position in particular, had little impact on the quality of education offered Brevard's students. I mostly shuffled paper between the schools and the county office, and vice-versa. When, in 1969, an interesting alternative presented itself, saying yes was easy. I was approached by editors from the publisher Prentice-Hall, Inc., and asked to help them salvage an elementary school-level social science textbook series. They had a great deal of money invested in the project, and at grade level three the authors had run out of ideas. They offered to match my salary with royalty advances if I'd take a leave of absence and write full-time.

It was a good deal. I was never actually employed by Prentice-Hall, but they were generous with royalty advances and pushed consulting business my way from other companies they owned. I terminated my leave of absence from the Brevard County school system and resigned. Over the next seven years I authored, with my brother Howard, an American History textbook, a world cultures textbook, Florida's social studies guide, and much other educational material.

Prentice-Hall also signed me to co-author a senior high school social studies series with Alvin Toffler. Toffler's *Future Shock* had just made the best seller list, and Prentice-Hall officials thought he and I would make a good team. His speaking engagements and my writing and consulting left time only for a few weekend meetings at his homes in Connecticut and Manhattan, and we never actually produced anything together, but it was fun, and a rich source of ideas.

In the mid-1970's, American education was swept by an ultra-traditional "back to basics" movement. My work certainly wasn't traditional in outward appearance, demand for the kind of work I was interested in doing declined, and I wanted to teach full-time again. I also wanted to stay near my children, build a house on the Indian River, and have more time to travel. Brevard Community College, less than 10 minutes away, was the most reasonable option. Then-BCC Liberal Arts Division Chair Robert Aitken had always been enthusiastic about my work as an adjunct. He offered me the position of Coordinator of Human Services Technology at the College, and I began work in the fall of 1977.

The Human Services Technology program was in disarray, and putting it in some sort of order occupied me for two or three years. Aitken had confidence in me, and I was left alone to set up procedures for selecting students, designing the instructional program, and working with local social service agency heads to place students in jobs. I liked to innovate, and the program offered ample opportunities.

It was my compulsion to try out new ideas that, little by little, raised my profile with the administration. As possibilities occurred to me, I'd submit proposals. When, days or weeks later, there had been no administrative response, I'd follow up with a request for a status report. I just couldn't accept Division Chair Aitken's insistence that new ideas—at least someone else's new ideas—weren't viewed positively by College President Maxwell King. It took me a long time (too long for my own good) to understand that proposals for change were interpreted as criticisms of the status quo, and criticism of the status quo was unacceptable. By the time I learned that Aitken was right, I was marked as a troublemaker. Although I'd never before belonged to a faculty union, the possibility that I might need legal protection led me to join.

TROUBLE

Once I realized that any attempt on my part to innovate was a waste of time, I joined most of the rest of the faculty in trying to ignore the administration and concentrate on my classes. Apparently, in King's view, this was as it should be. I recall a faculty member telling me what King had told him about the proper division of labor: "You teach, I'll run the College." That colleges, like all other institutions, are integrated systems in which everything relates to and has implications for everything else was a concept either not understood by King or else not acceptable to him.

What I saw as minor frictions notwithstanding, I occasionally put forward suggestions and reacted to what I felt were unsound educational policies. In the early eighties I wrote King a long memo protesting a new examination policy, laid out a plan for cooperation between the College and local social service agencies, had a run-in with the administration about my failure to use textbooks in my classes, proposed ways to open the College to non-traditional students, suggested that an outside consultant firm look at the depressed state of faculty morale, and asked lots of questions. Generally, however, I concentrated on my classes and on a book I was writing about curriculum theory.

In 1982, Division Chair Aitken was transferred from Cocoa to the Melbourne campus. Two or three years later, at his request, I transferred also.

The faculty at Melbourne was close knit, warm and supportive, a state I attributed in part to the fact that the campus was 20 miles from the administration building. Except for a couple of attempts by the central administration to use policy technicalities to harass me, the early years at Melbourne were uneventful.

But in the spring of 1988, stuff hit the fan. Construction of what was eventually to become the Maxwell C. King Center for the Performing Arts was underway amid much controversy. Into the middle of the fan's blast stepped Alecia Elbert, editor for BCC's student newspaper, the *Capsule*.

Alecia had written an editorial critical of the spending priorities she felt the construction of the performing arts center reflected, and of maintenance workers being pulled off campus duties to work on the new center. Part-time teacher and *Capsule* advisor George Thompson, remembering his promise to the administration to keep derogatory news about the College out of the school paper, told Alecia it was too hot for the *Capsule*. But he made her an offer. If she was willing, he'd take the editorial to *Florida Today* and see if they'd be interested in running it as a guest column. They were, and they did. Alecia's column, "**Community college cuts services to finance building binge,**" created an administrative storm. Alecia wrote:

> They may be broke, but they have lots of pretty buildings.
> Brevard Community College officials pride themselves on growth. Even their motto, "A place to grow," displays their need to be the biggest—if not necessarily the best.
> They are doing very well in their quest: Renovation of the Cocoa Village Playhouse, which they acquired for a dollar (who knows how much it will cost to maintain?); a new vo-tech center; an authentic Seminole Indian village; and last (but definitely not least) the Brevard Performing Arts Center. No doubt about it, they're looking good.
> One problem, however: During its "gotta be bigger" binge, BCC has all but wiped out quality in education. It has become something of a construction-monger, eating money and spitting out concrete. Students are being trampled in this feeding frenzy, lost among bulldozers and hard hats.
> Yes, the cuts are everywhere: Security, student assistants, the mini-mester, janitors, the *Capsule* newspaper, even the "Yummy-gram," a fun-filled, one-page xerox copy of the lunchroom menu . . .
> Students are singing the blues, all right—and they have every right to be. One example of the administration's lack of interest in us is the stu-

dent newspaper, the *Capsule*. Recently trans-
formed from a biweekly to a weekly publication,
it found itself in need of a few basic items, such as
computers, telephones and a scanner which would
cut production costs in the long run. The newspaper staff (students) applied for a grant.

But the administration held up that grant for
fear it might affect another grant concerning the
Arts Center. Now we're cutting the paper back to
bimonthly.

The bitter feelings are there. Students encoun-
ter them every time they enter a filthy bathroom.
(Yes, the janitorial staff has been cut, too.) . . .

BCC will continue to devour the countryside,
building and expanding until it bursts. We hear
now of plans to build a magnificently modern
swimming pool someplace on the grounds, obviously in place of the classrooms we need so badly.

It's a "place to grow," all right. Too bad it's
not the students who are doing the growing.

(Florida Today, *3-8-88)*

When the paper hit the stands, near-hysteria hit
upper-level administrators. BCC Vice President Robert
Anderson drove down to Melbourne, found Alecia, took
her into a private room, closed the door and, while other
students eavesdropped in consternation, confronted her in
such a way she was afraid for her physical safety.

"He made me sit down, stood over me, and waved his
finger in my face," she said. "He's a big guy. I was
afraid."

Freedom of the press wasn't a popular concept with
the BCC administration. The *Capsule* office was moved
immediately to the Cocoa campus and a friend of Vice
President for Student Affairs Bob Anderson was brought

from out-of-state to serve as the newspaper's advisor. Full-time faculty with journalistic experience and a willingness to advise the *Capsule* staff were given no opportunity to apply for the job. Despite his love of teaching, *Capsule* adviser, writer, broadcaster, retired Foreign Service officer George Thompson was never again offered a BCC class to teach.

A few weeks later, I wrote a letter to the editor of *Florida Today* saying that it would be unfortunate if, in focusing attention on Alecia's editorial, the larger problems of the College were ignored. I learned via the grapevine that King was extremely angry with me.

WHERE THERE'S SMOKE . . .

Sometime during the course of the ensuing controversy, Dr. King was quoted in *Florida Today* as saying, "This is a beautiful institution." I think this is what led to a decision by a group of faculty to determine to what extent the faculty shared his view. Perhaps, we speculated, Dr. King had been so successful in insulating himself, the trustees and the public from reality that just about everybody really did believe that all was well. After all, when plaudits for the administration seemed to cascade in non-stop from everywhere, it was reasonable to believe that opposition really was coming from "just a few disgruntled faculty." Maybe King was correct in his insistence that those who opposed him had "family problems," had "failed to meet personal goals," were "worried about their health," were "concerned about their marriages," were "involved in divorces," or had "antinuclear concerns." Psychologists on the faculty speculated that perhaps King was illustrating the psychological process called "projection"—attributing to others his own deep-seated states of mind.

Several teachers wondered what could be done to convince the community that BCC had extremely serious,
long-ignored problems. Just cataloging them seemed to be
a logical first step. So, quietly and informally, blank index cards were distributed. Faculty members asked other
faculty members to write down what was on their minds
about the College.

Reactions poured in. Much of it was redundant, but
the volume of responses and their range was startling.

A faculty group organized the items by subject, phras-
ing them as questions (since many of them dealt with
matters of which we knew little or nothing, and we didn't
want to make false accusations). We published a draft to
elicit additions, corrections and suggestions in preparation for a final version.

We called the document "Priorities." It began with a
quote from a state statute reminding the reader that the
primary purpose of the State's community colleges was to
educate, and only secondarily to provide the kinds of community services and tourist attractions for which King
seemed to be trying to make the College famous. It continued with a brief introduction:

> When a speech teacher's request for a simple
> lectern for student speaking is rejected year after
> year, but money can be found to pay a College
> bartender; when an offer by teachers to build
> their own offices if the college will furnish the
> materials for partitions is turned down citing lack
> of money, but $77,000 can be found to build a
> decorative canopy over the entrance to the admin-
> istration building; when the state mandates that
> every student in a class shall write a minimum of
> three thousand words, but the teacher responsible
> for evaluating that writing is assigned as many as
> one hundred seventy-five students; when there are

no available classrooms, but millions of dollars are spent on a building of very marginal educational utility; when (despite the President's never-ending words about "service to students") money to equip a biology lab is denied for eight consecutive years, serious questions are raised about the priorities of those in charge of the decision-making process.

(Exhibit #28)

Twelve single-spaced pages of probing questions followed, categorized by subject. The questions provide some insight into the kinds of matters that disturbed faculty. A small sample:

■ Have administrators who have been responsible for the acquisition of grants or other individual actions viewed as meritorious by the President been the recipients of $2,000 checks, quietly presented outside the usual payroll procedures? If so, who have the recipients been? For what reasons? From what funding sources?

■ A recent persistent rumor has it that, by request, certain highly paid administrators will retire before the next audit. Supposedly, they have been advised that their retirement will give the appearance of a reduction in the administrative component of the College and that they will be rehired as consultants on short-term contracts in order to promote this illusion. Has this procedure ever been used? Is it currently in use? Are there plans to employ this deception in the future? If the majority of these administrators are not to

be replaced, to what account have these dollars
been assigned?

■ On July 13, 1988, the President responded
to questions about the new light fixtures for the
production "Pioneers of the River Ridge." He
stated that "the lighting was borrowed from the
Performing Arts Center." If this is the case, why
was the check to Miami Stagecraft for the lights
written from the Cocoa Fine Arts Department
budget? Is it planned that monies for the Performing Arts Center will be "laundered" through various budgets for the coming year?

■ Have purchase orders ever been split in
order to bypass the bidding requirement?

■ What are College policies relating to nepotism in bid contracts? What guidelines are established to assure that the College will not violate
nepotism regulations in all areas? Are contracts
ever let to companies owned entirely or in part by
College personnel? If this has happened, what procedures were used to circumvent the policy?

■ What discretionary power does the President have over the expenditure of funds allocated
to the College? To whom does the President
answer concerning independent accounts that
have been registered as tax-free corporations
affiliated with Brevard Community College? How
many of these entities exist? Has yet another independent corporation been formed with the intent to commercialize, for profit, productions being
developed in the BCC Planetarium? Will any of
the profits realized from this venture be made
available for the instructional activities of the
College? Where can information about expenditures and income of the BCC Planetarium, the
BCC Foundation, the BCC Booster Club, and

other semi-autonomous organizations operating under the BCC umbrella be located?

■ Professional travel for faculty and staff is limited. However, few or no restrictions for travel appear to be placed on administrators or members of the Board. For example, Mr. Humphrys went to Hungary to visit just one teacher. Why? Board members and their spouses have recently returned from the annual workshop for Community Colleges for International Education in Vermont at a cost of about $1,000 per couple. How can such policies be justified? What procedures are in place for keeping such perquisites from compromising Board objectivity?

■ Some basketball players at BCC receive not only free books and tuition but also free meals in the cafeteria, $25 for weekends, and checks to pay their rent. What is the funding source for this accommodation? Is this the only group that receives such subsistence? If so, why don't other similar representative groups receive such help? What is the academic justification for aid as extensive as this for such a small number?

■ It is widely believed that irregularities in the maintenance department are routine—that the director of maintenance is part owner of a roofing company which receives a major part of College contractual work; that construction materials ordered for the College are sometimes diverted to private use; that air conditioners, generators, and other pieces of expensive equipment are sometimes removed from College vehicles and kept for private use before the vehicles are sold, thereby decreasing vehicle resale value; that employees have been given undocumented (therefore paid) "vacation" time to help in a supervisor's private business; that used heavy equipment has been

purchased by supervisory personnel and resold to
the College at an excessive profit; that private
businesses are run on BCC property using BCC
tools, facilities, equipment and utilities; that BCC
trucks have been used off campus on weekends in
an employee's private business; that parts from
donated cars have been removed and installed on
administrators' cars; that items such as cabinets
are sometimes custom built for administrators but
passed off as "class projects"; that the record of
success of certain individuals in submitting the
low winning bid for purchase of boats and other
donated items made to the BCC Foundation is
outstanding. Have any of these irregularities ever
been investigated?

■ The Wildlife Preserve located on Wickham
Road at I-95 in Melbourne was originally operated
by the county school system. What procedures
were used to cause the transfer of operations of
this property to the College? Why? What caused
its demise? Was the project consistently under-
funded, or was mismanagement the cause of the
community's loss of this facility?

(Ibid.)

"Priorities" concluded:

   Answers to our questions will not provide a
comprehensive accounting of the public monies en-
trusted to Brevard Community College; however,
we hope that public servants, sensing the nature
and level of concern that permeates the entire
institution, will insist that a public accounting of
intelligible data and a clear statement of the

philosophy, values and assumptions which govern
the kind and quality of education offered to the
students at Brevard Community College be made
available to the taxpayers of this county.

(Ibid.)

Although "Priorities" was written in draft form and
addressed to faculty for the purpose of revision and additions, King responded almost instantly. And predictably.
He called it "scurrilous literature," and told John Nagy,
a reporter for *Florida Today*, that he was "ashamed that
something like this is distributed within a professional
community." ("Professional" and "professionalism" are
two of King's favorite words. Whatever he likes is professional; whatever he dislikes is unprofessional.) Nagy's
September 15, 1988 article went on to quote King's decla-
ration that he wouldn't respond to any of the questions
because they were submitted anonymously.

That reaction had also been anticipated. On the front
cover of "Priorities," the following had appeared:

ON ANONYMITY

From the varied perspectives represented in
this document, it should be apparent that many
individuals have contributed. Without exception,
these individuals know that unsigned documents
are taken less seriously than those which are
signed. They are also aware, however, of the long
history here of intimidation and fear. Concern for
the College prompts them to raise the issues; concern for their jobs and the welfare of their fami-

lies prompts them to wait for a healthier, fairer
atmosphere before identifying themselves.

(Ibid.)

     Never mind all that, said the trustees, they backed
King in his refusal to respond.
     But, in fact, there was a response. Board chairman
Philip Nohrr agreed to meet on a Sunday afternoon in
the fall of 1988 with a delegation of "Concerned Faculty."
     The meeting was set for 3:00 p.m. at Rialto Place
near the Melbourne airport. Waiting for Nohrr at an
away-from-the-traffic side door, several members of the
delegation were sure they saw BCC administrator
Dr. Billy Nunn cruise by checking faces. "Dr. King,"
someone snickered, "now has a little list." No explanation was needed. As it turned out at annual faculty
evaluation time, King did indeed have a little list. And
we were all on it.
     The meeting was uneventful. Nohrr listened politely
to a long list of grievances and charges of corruption and
incompetence, but said almost nothing.
     A short while later, the faculty received an indirect
response to its charges that King's administration was
bankrupt. The trustees extended his contract for four
more years.
     As of this writing, nearly all the questions raised in
"Priorities" remain unanswered. None have been discussed in board meetings. Neither has any newspaper
printed anything indicating an effort to investigate actions many of which, if true, were felonious. Mike Lafferty, a reporter for the *Orlando Sentinel*, began an investigation of C&C Roofing, and told me that in a matter of
hours he had found evidence that the College had adver-
tised for bids primarily to domestic rather than commer-

cial roofing companies, thereby eliminating nearly all the competition. The one commercial roofer who did place a bid submitted it five minutes before the deadline and was told by the apparently innocent secretary that he was lucky because no other bids had come in. Nevertheless, C&C Roofing—an outfit rumored to be owned by the brother of Vice President Harold Creel, and perhaps by Creel himself, got the nod. Creel was in charge of deciding what roofs would be repaired and replaced. Faculty used to shake their heads in disbelief at the amount of carpet, furniture and equipment ruined by leaking roofs.

Sentinel reporter Lafferty thought there was enough material to keep a team of investigators busy for months. However, before he could proceed, the south Brevard mall shooting known as "The Palm Bay Massacre" took place. He was sent to Sanford to cover the trial, and at its conclusion was assigned to Osceola County.

MORE SMOKE

The matters referred to in "Priorities" had been phrased as questions, but that didn't mean that they were based on casual rumor. In addition to voluminous information provided by secretaries, maintenance workers, security personnel and other current or past employees with firsthand knowledge and a willingness to put ethical considerations above loyalty to the administration, there were paper trails.

Some matters were relatively insignificant, but reflected what most faculty considered a disturbing callousness toward students. A couple of the provisions of a College contract with an outside food vendor slipped to us by a helpful administrator illustrate the point:

5. Other Services to be provided:

a. Contractor agrees to provide coffee service to six (6) offices as directed by the College. Coffee service shall be defined so as to include the necessary brewing equipment and all coffee, tea, cream, sugar, stirrers, etc., as may be needed. Cost of this service shall be borne by the Contractor.

b. Over and above the cost to the Contractor for item 5a, the Contractor agrees to provide miscellaneous catering service to the College at no cost to the College up to a total value per year of $3,000 for items 5a and 5b combined.

c. Within the first year of operation, the Contractor agrees to provide and pay for a minimum of $50,000 of renovations to the College food service areas.

"Cost of this service shall be borne by the Contractor."

(BCC-Service America contract, 1988-91)

Only from a dulled ethical perspective could it be argued that coffee to those six very well-paid administrators, the free meals and the other benefits were compliments of the Contractor. Their costs were, of course, added to the price of hamburgers in the cafeteria.

On the first day of the "official" hearing to dismiss me, King, the trustees, two BCC lawyers, and a trustee wife or two, retired to King's conference room at lunch time. Through an open door, a table set with white tablecloth, china and silverware was visible. A few minutes later, sitting in the school cafeteria eating hamburgers with my lawyers and witnesses, I remembered the photocopied food service contract. How ironic. My "neutral" judges were having lunch with my accusers, and my students were paying the bill.

Failed to keep word to writer,

PJC President's credi

BY OBIE CRAIN
Special Projects Writer
Pensacola Press Gazette

The credibility of Pensacola Junior College President Dr. Horace E. Hartsell has failed to pass muster by his failure to keep his word to deliver information to this reporter.

NEITHER DID D̲r̲. H̲

have shifted between interviews with this writer.

Serious questions involving impropriety and possible criminal consequence have subsequently surfaced in *The Corsair*, the PJC student newspaper wherein the Equal Employment Opportunity

[forr
Inst

cont
repo
as w
teri
adm
ered
surf
the

PBCC gave rent receipts to private foundation

A state audit found the illegal practice had gone on for years.

■ In its annual report to the U.S. Department of Education, the college understated the amount received for tuition and fees by $1.2 million.

By DON HORINE
Staff Writer
Palm Beach Post

LAKE WORTH — Money col-
lected for renting athletic facili
at Palm Beach Comm
was routinely
college's n

'FCCJ

By Joan Henness
Staff Writer
Florida Times-Union

It was a simp
Foundation spend its
Betty Cook, a tr
at Jacksonville, wan
After all, the co
with

A good lesson in waste

A report shows Florida has hired far more administrators than teach

Audit asks: Did

By ROBERT SAMEK
Staff Writer
St. Petersburg Times
PENSACO

lisher

ity questioned

Second
pen
n

Frustrations prompt HCC trustee to quit

By STEVE KANIGHER
Staff Writer
Tampa Tribune

TAMPA — Banker Tony Salario said Thursday he will resign from the board of trustees of Hillsborough Community College because he does not have enough time to devote to the position, and also because he disapproves of some of the college administrative practices.

• • • •

tion to react quickly to the fact that its financial records have not been balanced since mid-1986, a problem HCC officials blame on faulty computer software.

"It's not good for any person or business to go for two years without reconciling your books," he said. "You just can't let it go."

He also said he was disappointed because the administration failed to provide trustees with a report detailing the reasons why certain adminis- led for merit

undation audit stirs unrest

club membership

Appointee to community college board leases to HCC

By STEVE KANIGHER
Staff Writer
Tampa Tribune

Thomas J. Murphy, 48, owns one-third interest in Pinebrooke Business Park, which HCC ha

n: How d

lorida Comm

llege enroll dead people?

rds and course descriptions at th
ns month
oot the bill for travel and

Too little of the foundation's money is being spent on students, Girardeau said.

Part II

TRAVEL AGENTS

I suspect that what I considered improprieties in the College's agreement with its food service supplier were nothing compared to what didn't meet the eye in the College's relationship with the company that handled the hundreds of thousands of dollars spent by BCC students for foreign travel every year. I raised questions about the matter in a letter to King written in September of 1988:

Dear Dr. King:

A few days ago a booklet called "Priorities" began circulating at BCC. In the September 14 board meeting, you referred to it as "trash" and "scurrilous," and said you did not intend to respond to anonymous documents. (It could be pointed out that the booklet was from faculty, to faculty, and that you have no reason to respond. However, that is not why I now write.)

You need but check your letter file to know that over the years I have not been reluctant to state my opinions openly, and place them over my signature. Consistent with that, I would like to comment concerning those specific questions in the booklet in which I have a special interest.

I sing in the Brevard Chorale on the Cocoa campus. A few months ago, Mark Hanson, our director, suggested the possibility of a concert trip to Europe. He said that he had checked, and that the cost would be about $2,800.

Joy and I go to Europe every year. We felt the
quote was high for the tour he described, so I
began to make inquiries, inquiries which eventually led me to [Dr.] Jeff Reynolds, choral director
on the Melbourne campus. Jeff had received information from a tour agency with which he had
worked on two previous occasions at another college, and with which he was happy. He had obtained the information before he was told that he
could not do that, that all foreign travel at BCC
was handled by CIE [Consortium for International
Education].

In summary form, here is a comparison of
BCC's CIE proposal and a firm offer from ETC of
Winchester, Virginia:

CIE	ETC
14 days	14 days
3 countries, all in close proximity to one another	6 countries, from England to Austria
5 tours, mostly walking	7 tours, transported; plus Danube cruise, plus tickets to Vienna opera
breakfasts; 5 dinners	breakfasts; 13 dinners
"O.K. to sing on steps of public buildings."	Concerts booked into appropriate facilities; press releases arranged; posters distributed
$2,265	$1,995

When Jeff asked for a CIE quote on a tour comparable to the $1,995 tour provided by ETC, but did not disclose that he already had in hand a guaranteed price from ETC, he was told "about $3,700." It is this sort of thing that convinces me that the questions raised in "Priorities" need to be asked. There may very well be a reasonable explanation for a nearly *double* price for comparable tour arrangements, but from the outside it is difficult to imagine what that explanation might be. Hence, the question.

I will be most interested in the answer, and how it will be received by the hundreds, perhaps thousands of individuals in this area who made or are making bank payments on loans taken out for BCC's travel abroad programs. Perhaps there is no legal requirement for annual competitive bids on each tour package, but surely we have a moral obligation to provide our students, a captive audience, with maximum benefits at minimum cost.

I cannot speak to any of the other issues raised in the booklet, I have not the slightest idea where they originated. But the apparent handling of this matter about which I have hard and direct information suggests that many of the other questions may also bear investigation. May I suggest that the answers to which we have become accustomed, that you "did not know what was going on," or that you "thought the problem had been taken care of," may, for some of the questions, prove to be less than adequate.

Additionally, I am enclosing samples of just a few budget data sheets [obtained under the table from an administrator] which raise questions about administrative priorities in a year when there is supposed to be no money.

I think all this is very sad. But when you
refuse to allow us to participate in any meaningful way in the functioning of this institution;
when you cut us off from meaningful communication; when you refuse our requests for board representation on committees such as the Blue Ribbon and the Liaison, we have no way to provide
the feedback that would keep situations like the
present one from arising.

(Exhibit #131)

King didn't call or respond on paper. In keeping with
his obvious policy of insulating himself from blame, he
sent Vice President Jim Humphrys to see me. At the
time, Humphrys was in charge of international education. We mostly sat and looked at each other. He offered
no explanation for the different price quotes from CIE
and ETC. He simply said that the College had dealt with
CIE for a long time, and the administration preferred
working with an organization with which it was familiar.
When I said that Professor Reynolds had used the other
company twice before coming to BCC and had been com-
pletely pleased with it, Humphrys said nothing.

CHILL THE CRITIC

I had moved from Cocoa to the Melbourne campus at
the specific request of Division Chair Robert Aitken. Subsequently, Aitken became provost of the Cocoa campus
and was replaced by Dr. Ann Thomas.

I've taught in full- or part-time positions in nine different institutions under a great many administrators. If
I had to choose the best of them all, Dr. Thomas would
probably be my choice. She was intelligent, firm, ex-

tremely knowledgeable about the College, kept up with the literature and with trends in both education and in management, was absolutely honest, had her priorities straight, and knew how to get the best from those who worked for her. Perhaps most appreciated was her ability to run interference through the bureaucracy. She made it possible to do worthwhile things in the face of administration-imposed obstacles. I never met any member of the faculty who had worked for her at Titusville, Melbourne or Cocoa who didn't think she was the most competent administrator at the College. Just about everyone agreed that, if the institution functioned as it ought to have functioned, she would have been its president.

Supervising me put Dr. Thomas and Dr. Elena Flom, her boss and provost of the Melbourne campus, over a barrel. Privately, they assured me they had no objection whatsoever to the positions I took. They certainly weren't willing to take any sort of disciplinary action against me for engaging in it. On the other hand, they were getting enormous pressure from King to shut me up. He and other upper echelon administrators couldn't offer any specific suggestions as to just how they were to do that, but that didn't stop the two of them from being held responsible. King's position was, "If you were good administrators, you'd figure out some way to do the job."

The job got done, at least for about a year, beginning in the fall of 1988. However, King probably wouldn't have understood the reason even if he had known what it was. Dean Thomas and Provost Flom didn't ask me to back off. Neither did they tell me that King had frozen their salaries to make certain they understood just how unhappy with them he was. I stopped writing letters to editors and otherwise speaking out in public simply because I hated to see them under so much unfair pressure.

As the time approached for administrative evaluations of faculty for the 1988 academic year, the heat was on not merely Drs. Thomas and Flom, but on all supervisors of suspected faculty activists. Dr. Perk Marquess, a provost-level administrator who was considered by many faculty to be King's head hatchet man, held a meeting with selected department heads. According to a participant, after saying, "This meeting didn't happen," Marquess identified certain faculty and asked which of them could be given lowered evaluations for 1988.

A short time later, Dr. Thomas called me into her office. She told me that she had spent hours wrestling with the wording of a "Narrative Summary of Performance" that had to accompany my evaluation. Marquess expected her to punish me. She was unwilling to do that, so she had to try to find wording that would sound harsh enough to balance her failure to actually grade me down on the individual evaluation scale items.

She asked me to read what she had written, and tell me if I was willing to sign it:

This evaluation covers the year 1988. During the past year, the faculty and the administration were especially conscious and concerned about the need for evaluating institutional philosophy and practices. Mr. Brady was active during this time and served on the College's Blue Ribbon Committee—an ad hoc committee formed to examine issues of concern to the College.

It was during this period that Mr. Brady questioned the philosophy of the institution and expressed dissatisfaction with the College's administration. In August, Mr. Brady was informed by the division chairperson in a meeting with Mr. Brady and the Provost of the negative impact his public comments were having on the public perception of the campus and the College.

After discussing his attitude toward the institution with Mr. Brady, he stated that he is committed to open participation at the College. Mr. Brady said he would work toward channeling his energies into strengthening the instructional program at the Melbourne campus.

I had considered giving Mr. Brady a Below Expectation (BE) on question number 8 of the Administrative Performance Review of Instructional Faculty; however, since the conference I have not observed Mr. Brady making comments which may be regarded as negative, and I have not seen any letters or documents on which his name appears. In my opinion, Mr. Brady is doing what he said he would do. Recently he was asked to serve on a major collegewide committee, Strategic Planning, where he is an active participant in helping to fulfill the responsibilities assigned to the committee.

Mr. Brady and I will continue to work together to ensure professionalism in all College responsibilities and activities of which he is a part.

(Exhibit #133)

It wasn't necessary to read between the lines to see the administration's attitude toward the First Amendment to the United States Constitution. However, I signed the document because doing so seemed to create the fewest problems for Dr. Thomas.

Janis Campbell and Charles Hatfield, two other Melbourne faculty members considered to be activists, were given similar evaluations by their division head, Paul Rehberg. They protested vigorously. Rehberg, unable to give them a plausible explanation of his action, and unwilling to tell them he had been pressured to do what he had done, backed off Hatfield and Campbell's lowered evaluations when they submitted grievances. Not long afterward, he was fired.

I took up the matter of King's pressure on mid-level
managers in a February 1991 memo to him:

In our recent meeting, I was much concerned
with making the point that, because people thrive
and grow on a healthy mix of rights and responsibilities, the College would be far more dynamic if
each campus enjoyed a much greater degree of
autonomy.

Perhaps it was my preoccupation with this
matter which led me to pass over without reaction
one of your rather casual observations. I woke up
this morning remembering it, and wish to make
a belated response.

I don't remember your exact words, but the
gist of them seemed to be that you couldn't help
but think that (most? many?) of my actions at
BCC were somehow traceable to failures on the
part of administrators on the Melbourne campus.
That would have to mean, of course, Drs. Flom
and Thomas.

I want to take issue with your implication.
Without exception, I have found Dr. Thomas and
Dr. Flom to be reasonable, fair, and absolutely
professional. In fact, my gradual realization that
you apparently hold them responsible for "controlling" me has done more to temper my attacks on
what I see as superficiality and lack of vision in
this administration than could any amount of
threat of intimidation. If their administrative
styles had been different, be assured that my effort to move this institution toward sounder educational policy and practices would have been far
more public than has been the case. This is not to
say that I approve of everything they do; it is to
say that I, like most people on this campus, have

little difficulty distinguishing policy initiated here and policy initiated in "A" [the administration] building, and do not hold it against our administrators when I detect subtle differences in their administrative styles. (I might mention in passing that many faculty take it for granted that Paul Rehberg was moved and then fired because of his less-than-enthusiastic carrying out of an unwritten order to "punish" two faculty signers of a letter to the trustees . . .)

(Exhibit #145)

In legal terminology, the relevant question under the First Amendment to the Constitution is whether or not an action has a "chilling effect" on free expression. At BCC, policies and practices having such an affect are so much a part of institutional life that I suspect most faculty no longer understand what is and what isn't a flagrant violation of the Constitution.

I didn't stop working for change while attempting to shield Thomas and Flom, I just asked others to front actions I thought were important. This lasted for about a year. I think it ended on the day Dr. Thomas got a call from an upper level administrator telling her that I had been seen at *Florida Today* offices at lunch time and that she should do something about it. What she did was tell me that she was fed up with the whole thing, and that I should write and say anything I pleased.

WHAT'S YOUR OPINION?

To Dr. King's insistence that there were no problems at the College, the faculty had responded with a twelve-page list. Suppose, the faculty argued, that every one of the questions raised could have been traced to faculty ignorance or misperception. Wasn't faculty confidence in the integrity of the administration sufficiently important to warrant an attempt to allay the suspicions? Weren't faculty assumptions about incompetence and corruption an enormous problem standing in the way of institutional vitality? How could an institution be healthy and productive, we asked, when so many of those within it believed, rightly or wrongly, that its leadership was unworthy of respect?

Except perhaps as catharsis, "Priorities" had apparently been a waste of time. In Florida's community colleges, the trustees are the beginning and the end of the law. If they refuse to act (and, of course, they did), there's no action. Period.

Late in the year King came to the Melbourne campus to tidy things up with a kind of "status report." No one recorded what he said, but immediately afterward, about a dozen faculty pooled their recollections of his responses to questions.

King felt that:

■ it had been a difficult six months, but the major problems were behind us.

■ Whatever the problems, they were largely of our own making, or were due to middle-level manager ineptness, or were traceable to union tactics, or were the fault of the performing arts center architect, or stemmed from state mandates. His administration was blameless.

■ Given the rate of technological change, it wasn't possible for the College to equip itself. However, that wasn't a problem because it was theory that was most important, and theory could be taught without equipment.

■ There was no reason to be disturbed by the quality of the student newspaper because students did it.

■ Research had established that there was no difference in the quality of student advising offered by counselors and that offered by program advisors. [Counselors have master's degrees; most program advisors have community college degrees.]

■ What appeared to be cooperation between the faculty union and the administration at Miami-Dade Community College was an illusion, that what was really happening was that the union was taking over. At Brevard, cooperation between the faculty and the administration would begin when the union was abolished.

■ BCC's administration and faculty weren't capable of bargaining directly with each other, but needed the advice of Jesse Hogg, the administration's lawyer. Jesse's fees weren't secret, but he wouldn't, he said, disclose them.

■ The College was in excellent financial condition. Librarians and word processor personnel who were saying their funds had been radically cut were misinformed.

■ He was not and never had been vindictive.

■ Marion Brady's comments should be ignored by others just as they were ignored by him.

■ If a long-requested biology lab had not been funded, it was because programs, not individuals, should submit requests.

■ He got better results working one-on-one than with groups.

■ There should be two of him, because his problem-solving skills were so superb.

"Priorities" had failed. What next?

King never tired of maintaining that nearly everybody at the College was just short of deliriously happy. His claim that all the trouble could be traced to a few people like me suggested a survey to check out his allegation.

I had several times proposed to Provost Kay Heimer that the administration conduct such a survey. I had even offered to sign a pledge that if, on a secret ballot, just half the faculty said they had confidence in the administration, I'd shut up, not just for the moment, but permanently. She wouldn't buy it. Insisting that she saw no evidence at all of low morale, she said an administration-sponsored questionnaire was out of the question. It was clear that, if there was to be a survey, we'd have to do it ourselves.

There were lots of problems with that. First, we had to poll the faculty in a way that would be accepted as credible by a neutral observer. We decided to retain an attorney to collect and tally responses and announce results. Jim Hooper, an ex-chairman of BCC's trustees, suggested Kurt Erlenbach of Titusville. We contacted him and he agreed.

The second problem stemmed from the level of fear that permeated the College. So many faculty were afraid that their ballots would fall into administration hands that we had to work out an elaborate, double-envelope system to try to reassure them. One teacher, an extremely vocal activist before being put through a King kangaroo court and deprived of his tenure, was so fearful that, in spite of the safeguards, he refused to mail his survey form. He said he thought it entirely possible that Erlenbach's office would be broken into and the ballots stolen.

Approximately half the faculty responded. Attorney Erlenbach appeared before the trustees in a February 1989 meeting and, on behalf of "Concerned Faculty," read a statement:

Over the past year we have made a determined effort, both as individuals and as a group, to talk to you. As your employees, we feel we should have that privilege. We also feel that your understanding of the institution for which you are responsible could only be enhanced by closer contact with those of us who must carry out the policies you establish.

We were elated last fall when Mr. Nohrr indicated in *Today* newspaper his willingness to meet with us. His subsequent message, that such a meeting violates law, was extremely disappointing, the more so because, insofar as we can determine, the law does not prohibit such meetings. Mr. Nohrr has informed us that, if we wish to communicate with the Board, we have no alternative but to do so at one of its formal meetings. We regret the necessity for this very public airing of our problems, but that is the choice of the board.

We also regret that we must be represented by an attorney. However, history suggests that this is necessary. Many among us have learned from bitter experience that to express views about the College that conscience demands be expressed is to invite eventual administrative reprisal. Before union intervention, reprisal often meant being assigned classes on the campus farthest from one's home. Most recently, it has meant the use of threatening language on annual evaluations, the argument being that to criticize the administration is to criticize the College, that criticizing the College is unprofessional, and that unprofessional behavior should be punished. In the past, poor evaluations have preceded probation and deprivation of tenure.

Our view is that we have not only a right, but
a moral obligation to oppose that which we feel is
wrong, or inimical to the health and well-being of
the College and our students. We have come to
ask you to reconsider your refusal.

(Exhibit #132)

There followed a list of 15 agenda items we wanted to
talk about with the trustees.

Attorney Erlenbach then announced the results of the
survey: 29% said they had confidence in the president's
leadership ability; 67% said they didn't; 4% abstained.

The final tally left no doubt that far more than a
small, vocal minority had no confidence in the administration. The administration, of course, said the whole
procedure was fixed.

NEW FACE

During the period when arrangements were being
made to conduct the survey, Dr. Bert Purga was hired to
fill the College's number two position—Vice President for
Instruction. He was young and personable, and came
across as genuinely interested in doing some good. Early
on, I met him for lunch at Ashley's Cafe in Rockledge.

We talked at length. He looked me in the eye (I
learned he was good at that) and listened.

A short time later, still believing he'd be a positive
force for good at the College, I wrote him a lengthy memo
I hoped would help him survive BCC's minefields and do
some good. (I hadn't yet heard that Machiavelli was his
"hero.") Along with much else, I discussed the need to
admit that real problems existed, suggested that clear,
honest answers to faculty questions were necessary to

alter faculty perceptions of the administration, and said that denial and scapegoating were empty strategies getting us nowhere. I concluded:

> You've been at the College only a very short time. No doubt, however, that's sufficient for you to have been told that I'm a troublemaker. I ask you to experiment with a different label. Think of me simply as a source of information about what most of the faculty would be saying if they were willing to be hassled . . .
> Where am I "coming from"? That's easily answered. One: I take the responsibilities of tenure seriously. Two: I'd like, before I retire, to see some substance behind the incredible public relations facade that's been so artfully constructed here. Three: Much that I do is designed to convince faculty and staff that improvement is possible. Four: I won't take off my hat and shuffle my feet to get what fairness says my students and I deserve.

(Exhibit #184)

Purga's predecessor, Dr. Willis Holcombe, left BCC to become president of Broward Community College. In the years he was Vice President for Instruction at Brevard, we became friends, and over lunches and dinners we talked a great deal about the College. I won't disclose the content of those private conversations, but they made me appreciate the incredible difficulty of the position he was in, difficulty stemming from Dr. King's management style.

Primarily as a consequence of those conversations, when Purga came I was willing to cut him quite a lot of

slack. I appreciated the fact that he had a wife, kids, a
new house and a career to protect and maintain.

He took up the slack pretty quickly. A couple of
months after I sent him my memo, he was sitting near
the front of the Fine Arts auditorium listening—along
with the entire faculty—to Dr. King's familiar speech
marking the opening of the new school year. At its conclusion, Purga jumped to his feet and attempted to lead
the faculty in a standing ovation.

I should have known that all BCC administrators—
unless they were skillful manipulators—were powerless.
Years before, I'd watched a meeting in which administrators stalled, backed, and filled until they thought they
could read King's opinion, then they all came down solidly in agreement with him. At the time, I didn't know
whether to laugh or cry. Every decision of consequence,
and many inconsequential ones, were made by King.
Those he didn't make were invariably designed to second-
guess him.

MORE NEW FACES

Increasingly I realized that, if there was any hope at
all for change at BCC, it lay with the trustees. Once I got
this through my head, I began to pay much closer attention to the trustee selection process.

In my initial naivete, I had supposed that governors
appointed people who had at least a little understanding
of education and a passing interest in its quality.

Wrong. Community college trustee positions are
patronage plums handed out to reward or attract political
support, and as such are subject to manipulation by
lobbyists. In fact, according to a 1993 article in *Florida
Today*, at least three of the five BCC trustees sitting at
the time the article appeared had been funneled into
their positions by paid-BCC lobbyist Guy Spearman. In

what seems to me to be a rather incestuous relationship, lobbyists help select community college trustees, who then vote to retain the lobbyists. (In late April of 1994, Andrew Spilos, a young Melbourne Beach resident who had tried to collect information about this and similar cozy lobbyist-trustee arrangements, was sued by lobbyist Guy Spearman for "willfully and wantonly . . . causing injury and damage" to his (Spearman's) "reputation and business relationships." Spilos was arguing that the King-Spearman-Wasdin-Kirschenbaum-Stottler-Foley Construction-etc. relationships gave new meaning to the verb "networking."

Given my new appreciation of the community college trustee role, it was with considerable interest that, in 1989, I learned of the appointment of Dr. Frank Williams to the board. I had earlier met at length with Artie, Frank's wife, and urged her to seek the position. I knew her to be strong and independent. She had been interested, but my ally in the power structure hadn't been able to pull it off.

Frank Williams and I went way back. He was one of the first people I met when I came to Brevard County from Tallahassee in 1967. We shared an office at the old school board facility on U.S. 1 in Titusville.

A third person in the office was Bill McEntee. Bill had been head of inservice education for Brevard's public schools, but in the early '80's had moved to the College and was now a fellow member of the faculty.

McEntee and I talked about the possibilities. At last, we thought, someone who'll listen. Maybe even understand. And someone through whom we could get our concerns about College problems on record.

We called Williams and made arrangements to visit him at his home in Titusville. He welcomed us graciously. We sat in the living room and remembered old times, talked about old friends, laughed at old stories. The meeting went well.

Went well, that is, until we got around to BCC and the responsibility he was about to assume. Williams' mood changed almost instantly. The hostility was palpable. Our visit ended abruptly and we left. Driving back to Cocoa, Bill and I went over and over the experience. Neither of us had a clue to an explanation of Frank's reaction to us.

I sometimes learn slowly. It had taken a long time to realize that the key to improvement at the College was the trustees. It took another interval before I realized that, once in place, trustees are apparently unreachable. Why? I really don't know. Ask any half-dozen faculty and there'll be a half-dozen different answers: "They know so little about what they're doing they're easily snowed by administrative razzle-dazzle," "They're involved in behind-the-scenes business deals," "They're bought off by petty power and perks," "How could they know what's going on when they refuse to talk to anyone except King?" and, "They don't care."

Florida TaxWatch said that the job was just too big and complex for trustees operating without staff independent of the administrations for which they were responsible.

My growing appreciation of the key role of the trustees and the impossibility of working with them once they took office led me to later find out from the governor's office who the candidates were for the next openings.

In the spring of 1990, I went down the list, visiting all of them except Patrick Healy. I called him. He said he didn't think there was a chance he'd be chosen. In the event that he was selected, he implied that he had a mind of his own.

Besides personally visiting everyone I thought might be a trustee appointment, I wrote letters to key legislators and the governor:

66666

Dear Governor Chiles:

Faculty members at Brevard Community College know that, given the magnitude of most problems confronting you and the State, our problem is small potatoes. We also know however that, unlike many of the challenges you face, you can deal with this one quickly, at no cost, and with enormous potential benefit to thousands of students and the taxpayers of Brevard County.

Here's all we ask: In May [1990], Brevard Community College has two openings for trustees. Fill them with people who (a) know something about education, (b) understand budgets, (c) don't confuse public relations chaff with solid program, (d) are willing and able to spend time on campus with faculty and staff so as to determine problems and needed policies for themselves.

In a recent poll, 84% of faculty disagreed with the statement, "The policy-making level of administration at BCC is trustworthy, honest and reliable." We can't imagine that any leader with that level of follower confidence can be effective. An actively functioning board of trustees could begin to look into the root causes of this massive disaffection.

We're not asking for trustees who will be faculty mouthpieces. We're asking for trustees willing to ask tough, important questions about institutional operation, and decide for themselves what constitutes satisfactory answers . . .

(Brady Hearing Exhibit #63)

When the next appointments were announced, Patrick Healy was one of them. The other, Rachel Moehle, wife

of the governor's local campaign chairman, hadn't been
on the list I was given.

THE "PEPC" CHALLENGE

But I'm getting ahead of my story.
I can't remember how I learned of it, but late in 1989
it came to my attention that the Post-Secondary Education Planning Commission (PEPC) was touring the state
holding hearings on the subject of higher education
governance. PEPC is a creature of Florida's legislature.
Its members are appointed by the governor and charged
with making recommendations for the improvement of
higher education in the state.
I called PEPC's office, learned that they were meeting
on the 12th of December at a hotel near the Orlando airport, and asked to be put on the agenda.
Fellow faculty member Bill McEntee volunteered to
go with me to the meeting.
The PEPC commissioners sat at a table in the front
of a large meeting room on the first floor of the hotel.
The room was packed, and many people were on the
agenda. Since my presentation was lengthy, and I had
brought copies for everyone, I decided to go to the microphone, make a few general comments about community
college governance, and give the Commissioners my
handout to read on their own time. My memo wrapped up
just about everything I felt was wrong with the system.
I began by stating the problem:

My contention is a simple one: The state has
created, in the community college presidency, a
position of power with inadequate countervailing
checks and balances.

From every part of the state examples could be
cited of unchecked presidential power and of its
adverse effect on institutional health and instructional quality. Just in recent weeks, for example,
a community college president has resigned in the
wake of disclosures of unacceptable business dealings, dealings apparently unknown even to a state
legislator serving on that same president's staff.
It should be noted that it was not established
state procedures but the newspaper which uncov-
ered the presidential activity leading to the resignation.

(Exhibit #138)

I then laid out, in hypothetical terms, the dilemmas
faced by a faculty working with an administration it considered corrupt. Where were whistleblowers to go, I
asked, when the administration refused to respond, the
trustees wouldn't listen, the State Board of Community
Colleges claimed it had no jurisdiction, the local media
seemed to be in bed with the College's administration,
local legislators were afraid of losing campaign support
or were involved in business deals with administrators,
and law enforcement officials offered nothing but excuses?

Several pages later, I concluded with four suggestions.
I said, first, that although I wasn't an enthusiastic fan of
elected trustees, I was sure that the taxpayers would be
better served by them than by political appointees.

Second, I advocated periodic performance reviews of
community college presidents by those who knew them
best—their faculties, staffs and fellow administrators.

Third, I said there should be formal, institutionalized
channels of communication between trustees and college
employees through which trustees could get more accu-

rate pictures of the true state of the institutions for which they were responsible.

Finally, I pointed out that "as the economies of European east bloc nations amply demonstrate, centralized decision making simply cannot cope with the complexities of modern institutions. Community colleges are, of course, smaller than nations, but because what they are attempting is inherently more difficult than regulating production and distribution, the challenge is equally great." I said that moving community college decision-making mechanisms from "socialistic" to "capitalistic," from authoritarian to participative, was no less a challenge than that now faced in Eastern Europe, but the task needed to be undertaken, and for the very same reasons, that we were as backward and bankrupt educationally as Eastern Europe was economically.

What was needed, I said, was "a major study of new decision-making mechanisms within community colleges—mechanisms making it impossible for authoritarian leaders to mold institutions in their narrow images," because institutional vitality demanded nothing less than the harnessing of the vast collective power and wisdom of all participants in the community college educational process—students, faculty, staff, administrators and public.

McEntee and I left the hotel and went home. Six days later, on the 18th, I got a cryptic note on the letterhead of Kerrigan, Estess and Rankin, attorneys at law in Pensacola. It was signed "Robert G. Kerrigan," and said simply, "Would you please call me at your convenience?" The name was vaguely familiar, but I couldn't place it.

I called Kerrigan. He told me that he was one of the PEPC commissioners, that he had been present at the hearing in Orlando, and that I had given him a copy of my presentation. He said he was studying it carefully, but that that wasn't why he had asked me to call. The reason he wanted to talk to me, he said, was because of an incident at the hearing. He had discovered that, almost as soon as I had finished my presentation, one of the PEPC commissioners had faxed a copy of my remarks from the hotel to the president of my college. Kerrigan said he was appalled at the action, ashamed for the Commission, and had let everyone connected with PEPC know how he felt. (His comments to PEPC staff must have had quite an impact. Five years later I had occasion to call the PEPC office in Tallahassee. When I identified myself, the voice on the other end said, "Oh, I know who you are." Sure enough, they did.)

During my call to Kerrigan, he apologized on the Commission's behalf, and told me that if I ever suspected repercussions from my action that I should let him know. We've never met, but he's forwarded me some useful information, and has asked to be kept abreast of developments in my case.

The administration, the trustees, the State Board of Community Colleges, the governor, the media, the Florida Department of Law Enforcement—and now, even at least one unidentified PEPC Commissioner. When King said we couldn't hurt him because he had friends in high places, he obviously wasn't kidding.

ROBIN HOOD IN REVERSE

Many won't believe it, but I hate confrontation, and am usually rather good at finding alternative ways to deal with problems. I certainly never went looking for trouble at BCC. As I noted earlier, what happened is that, after a couple of letters to newspaper editors, a guest column or two, and a few direct questions to King and other administrators in College meetings and memos, I began to get letters and phone calls. Faculty and staff, and even a surprising number of administrators, apparently decided that if I were foolish enough to ask sensitive questions out loud, they'd let me.

So they fed me a steady stream of material, I'd ask the questions, and the asking would notch my profile up a little higher, bringing more questions to ask.

In the spring of 1990, faculty member Dr. Neil Hamilton told me that a campus security guard with whom he had gotten acquainted wanted to talk to me. Arrangements were made and, after assurances that I'd protect his identity, the security officer told me that he often worked far more than the legal 35 hours per week, with no overtime and no benefits.

I told him I'd need documentation, and he said that was a problem, that anything he could get would have his name on it.

I contacted a friend I thought might be able to help, and a few days later received a bundle of copies of completed time sheets involving enough different employees to make it impossible to pinpoint blame. There was even a copy of a handwritten note to one of the security guards reminding him that he had erred in putting down the hours he had actually worked, and saying that his "error" had been corrected, with the extra time pushed into the following week.

A glance at the time sheet format verified that the College's exploitation of security guards was done knowingly and intentionally. The sheet was titled, "SECURITY CARRY OVER TIME." The last column on the right read, "TOTAL CARRY OVER TIME REMAINING."

One of King's charges against me had always been that, whenever I came across something I thought was wrong, I went screaming to the media rather than working within the system. I had enough signed letters to him in my file to know that wasn't true, but I thought I'd play the game again to see what would happen.

Board Chairman John Henry Jones's office was about five minutes from my home. I called him, made an appointment, and took some of the documentation with me. I explained the problem, and told him that I was giving him an opportunity to deal with it rather than immediately going public.

I can't say now how long I waited to see if the trustees were going to act, but I'm sure it was several weeks.

When it became obvious that nothing was going to be done to remedy the situation, I went to Congressman Bill Nelson's office to find out what bureaucratic path it was appropriate to follow. He told me to put the problem in writing, and he'd see that it went where it needed to go.

I did. On the 21st of May, 1990, I wrote to him:

Thank you again for the assistance provided by your office. The numbered items below summarize the relevant information about the employment of part-time security guards by Brevard Community College beyond the weekly maximum allowable hours for part-time employees as established by federal statute.

Written, original records are available to verify that:

1. Week after week, part-time employees have worked in excess of sixty hours.

2. Not infrequently, weekly hours for a single employee have exceeded eighty.

3. No overtime monies are paid.

4. None of the benefits provided full-time employees have at any time been made available.

5. Security guards are required each week to sign statements that hours worked have not exceeded thirty-five.

6. Security guards who have entered on their time cards the actual number of hours worked in a week have had their cards altered by supervisory personnel to show only the allowable thirty-five

hours, and have been notified in writing that such
alteration has taken place.

   7.   At least a dozen part-time security personnel have worked under these circumstances.

   8.   The procedures have been in effect for over
a decade.

All the above can be verified either by written,
original records, or by photocopies of originals. A
sample time sheet filled out by a security guard
and a copy of the form which must be signed are
enclosed.

Thank you again for your willingness to assist
in this matter.

(Exhibit #142)

In less than two weeks, I got a call from Frank Dean,
an investigator for the Wage and Hour Division of the
National Labor Relations Board. He told me he'd be initiating an investigation within the next few days.

I heard from him every few weeks, the final time just
before I left the Brevard area in the fall of 1990 on a
leave of absence to do consulting work in Texas. Dean
told me that the problem was far more widespread than
I had supposed, and that he was still interviewing employees.

The investigation concluded while I was in Texas. In
November, my wife mailed me a clipping from *Florida
Today*. Following the headline, "BCC: Workers Under-
paid Nearly $18,000," reporter Jim Ash wrote, in part:

Four months after the U.S. Labor Department
ordered Brevard Community College to figure out
how much it underpaid its workers, college officials say they have an answer.

Between July 1, 1988, and July 1 of this year, 50 employees were underpaid $17,986, officials said.

"I think it's important to note here that we were not assessed a fine," said Bob Craig, BCC's Director of employee relations. "This is simply what we should have paid the employees all along had we known to do so."

Had they known to do so? **Had they known to do so?**

Of course they had known to do so. The forms used by the College tracked "carry over" time in a clearly labeled final column. And I had a copy of a note from a supervisor actually altering an employee's time sheet to make it "legal."

Richard Parham, the last full-time security guard at the College, told me about an occasion when Vice President Bob Anderson, at the time in charge of campus security, saw the new time-keeping form for the first time. He seemed a little taken aback, then said, "Hey, this is against the law." However, the forms continued in use until the federal investigation.

I had supposed that the closing of the investigation would end the matter. In fact, in the guise of cleaning up the mess, the College's administration generated more. Two years later, in November of 1992, I would find myself writing a letter to Bill Nelson's successor, Representative Jim Bacchus, on the same matter. In the letter, I briefly summarized the 1990 investigation, concluding with:

Mr. Dean eventually informed me that violations at the College were, in fact, more widespread than I had supposed. After extensive inter-

views, he allowed the College to plead ignorance
of the law and settle with employees either by
paying back wages or allowing use of "comp
time." The case was closed in the winter of 1990.

I then explained that, although I had thought the
whole matter was behind me, I had discovered that, in
"righting" earlier wrongs, the administration had continued its abuse of employees:

   1. Enormous pressure was put on employees
to forgo cash and settle for comp time. In addition
to verbal insistence by administrators that employees not ask for cash, the form provided by the
College contained a blank space only to indicate
hours. A request for cash had to be written in in
longhand, and no space to do so was provided.
   2. Many employees were "laid off" until the
amounts paid were recouped by the College. For
example, personnel who would ordinarily have
provided campus security were simply told to stay
home. Campuses were left without security, and
security personnel lost the wages they would ordinarily have earned.
   3. Employees who, despite the pressure, asked
for monies due them, were subsequently "reorganized" out of their jobs.

I said that I had been told by employees that the practice which brought the original action continued, albeit
on a smaller scale. [As far as I know, as of this writing,
nothing has been done about the continuing violations.]
It's interesting to speculate about the size of the settlement if someone had been mugged on one of the Col-

lege's parking lots or if there had been a medical emergency and, in an ensuing investigation, it became known that BCC had not had a single security guard on duty.

Of course, given the way the system works, the size of a settlement wouldn't have made any difference to anyone except the taxpayers. No matter how dishonest or irresponsible the action of community college administrators, if they're sued in their professional capacities, it's the taxpayers who pick up the tab.

Ethics Commission censu
Non-disclosure of Xepapas link cit

By MICHAEL HAWTHORNE
Capital Bureau
Daytona Beach News-Journal

TALLAHASSEE — Former Daytona Beach Community College President Charles Polk should be publicly reprimanded for failing to disclose his relationship with a developer doing business with the school,

the state Ethics Commission ruled Friday.

forced now West "I

Palm Bea
Board of Tr
Edward M. L
to talk to only
matters conce

Spence's travels lan
FCCJ in controversy

By Joan Hennessy
Staff Writer
Florida Times-Union

Charles Spence, like Benjamin Wygal, has seen the world.

But largely because of it, Wygal lost his job in 1984 as president of Florida Community College at Jacksonville.

Spence, who replaced him, has been away from the college the equivalent of 175 working days during the past three years.

He has seen the world — France, England, Russia, Canada and more — at the expense of the taxpayers

very lonely. It's stressful. And I have the good of the college."

Not everyone sees it that way.

At least two FCCJ board membe whether there's any benefit to the college.

And the news is ill-timed for stud tions about Spence's travel come at th troubled economic year that began cutting 330 classes in the face of st shortfalls.

Meanwhile, over a three-year peri has attended about 40 ciation

PJC audit could
return of funds to

Polk

sign in July 1989. H
t of the College o

board had better do
nsure there is public
ne system,"
ired educ
res w

SPJC president is charged with holding illegal meetings

St. Petersburg Times

CFCC dealings will be studied

By CHRISTOPHER B. JONES
St. Petersburg Times

A — Central Florida Community College has
and received items from companies that employ
esident William
other college
the St.

munity College
President
tells trustees
about
he college.

HCC audit woes amaze official

By STEVE KANIGHER
Staff Writer
Tampa Tribune

DAVIS ISLANDS — A state official says Hillsborough Community
College's computer-related problems
are the worst he has seen in 20 years
on the job.

• • •

oblems was an
e of $63,138
statements and

its general ledger. The audit also
cited a lack of adequate accounting
controls in such areas as college in-
vestments and student financial aid.

Because Florida's community
colleges are locally controlled by independent boards of trustees, [budget
and accounting administrator for the
state Division of Community Colleges
Ken] Jarrett said the state's authority
to enforce specific audit recommendations may be limited.

rce
tate

orks

Part III

IMAGE AND REALITY

I had criticized administrative policy and unresponsiveness, helped organize a confidence vote, written a letter supporting Alecia Elbert, helped publish an index of allegations of corruption, addressed the Post-Secondary Education Planning Commission, written guest columns about the College's administration in *Florida Today*, gone public with BCC violations of federal labor laws.

My wife started standing well back when I turned the ignition key in the car. I'm not sure she was kidding.

Faculty hammered away. However, despite our best effort, we suspected that the media and the public still believed that, on balance, the College was well run. To the casual observer, the most reasonable explanation of the situation was that King was a great educator who had the misfortune of being saddled with a faculty incapable of catching his vision.

The public image was understandable. At regular intervals, the newspapers carried articles about new honors heaped on the institution and on Dr. King. Representatives of local groups marched through trustee meetings in a near-continuous line with plaques and laudatory proclamations. Foot-high letters on the marquees of the county's American Banks once spelled out for an entire month, "WE SALUTE DR. MAXWELL KING, THE NATION'S TOP COLLEGE ADMINISTRATOR."

What the general public didn't know about was the time, money and effort invested by the College's public relations department in orchestrating King's awards and honors. What those driving by the county's American Banks probably didn't know was that King was on American's board of directors. What most citizens probably didn't guess was that King had bested the presidents of Harvard, Yale, Stanford, Notre Dame, MIT, and all other colleges and universities in the nation only in the opinion of a little outfit out in Tuscaloosa, Alabama. The criteria upon which their opinion was based weren't made public. (A Broward faculty member told me that Hugh Adams, pushed out of the presidency of Broward Community College by the faculty and the local legislative delegation because his performance was intolerable, had gotten the same "top administrator" award the year before he was deposed.)

Image. That's what it was all about. State Senator Bud Gardner, at the time a real powerhouse in Florida's legislature, told me that, as long as King maintained his public image, we were wasting our time in trying to end his tenure. Confronted by a public relations juggernaut operating full-time with a $100,000-plus budget, and with instant access to the media, what could the faculty do?

There weren't many options. We finally decided to conduct a carefully controlled, sophisticated, high-profile faculty survey. For those genuinely interested in reality as distinct from image, what better source for the straight story than a couple of hundred well-educated people who worked with the administration every day? College faculties almost never totally agree on anything. If we all harmonized about the College's administration, surely the song would be heard and the legislative delegation, the media, the public—somebody—would demand action.

This time, we wouldn't just go for a straight up or down confidence vote; we'd try to get a clear picture of **why** people felt as they did. This time, we'd use professionally prepared survey forms and questions, and run them through the administration so that they couldn't later say that the survey was biased or slanted. This time, we'd keep the media informed of what we were doing as we went along. And this time, instead of having a lawyer present the findings to a hostile board of trustees, we'd go public with a professionally done press release.

We spent weeks polishing the six-part survey. Batteries of questions were designed to probe faculty opinion on the union, wages and benefits, the College's physical environment, professional concerns and the administration. (Because of the sensitivity of the section evaluating the administration, it was lifted verbatim from a textbook on the subject, Richard I. Miller's *Developing Programs for Faculty Evaluation*, published by Jossey-Bass.) The survey concluded with an opportunity for open-ended comment.

The instrument was first printed in draft form and widely circulated for comment and criticism. A cover note on the copies sent to the trustees informed them of our intent to conduct the survey, and said, "We'd like to think that, as our employer, you have an interest in us, and in factors affecting the quality of our classroom performance." Following some information about the logistics of survey administration, we concluded our note to the trustees with:

> Please let us know if you feel that any of the questions are inappropriate or unfair either in content or in presentation. We would also appreciate any suggestion you may have for additional questions touching on areas helpful in the pursuit of our shared goal of achieving institutional excellence.

> *(Brady Hearing Exhibit #59)*

The trustees didn't respond.

The survey was sent to 223 full-time BCC faculty members—both union and non-union—in March, 1990. One

hundred-forty-five responses were received—an extra-
ordinarily high return rate, and far more than necessary
to establish the survey's validity. The results were
compiled by a large committee, translated into easy-to-
read bar graphs contrasting negative and positive
responses, and released in April.

There were interesting, revealing responses to its 75
questions. In "Part One: The Union," 86% of faculty
agreed with the statement, "Union activity may bring
administrative reprisal." This probably explained why
only 52% thought it was acceptable to picket for issues
they considered important. Asked on one item if they
"stood up for" issues they believed in, 89% of faculty said
that they did. (I spent quite a lot of time speculating
about the significance of that response.)

In "Part Three: Physical Environment," the bar representing disagreement with the statement "Leaks,
noise, temperature are not problems" just about went off
the end of the scale.

Under "Part Four: Professional Concerns," 92% disagreed with the statement, "Committees are well
thought-out and effective." (At BCC, the administration
chooses the membership of important committees and
usually determines the leadership.) Asked if new ideas
were encouraged, and adequate provision made for evaluating and implementing them, 89% said no. Paralleling
this response, 80% disagreed with the statement, "The
College has shown continuous qualitative improvement
over the years," and 85% disagreed with the statement,
"The institutional atmosphere is dynamic, enthusiastic,
and exciting." Only 14% thought that "Qualified administrative assistance for evaluating and implementing programs (was) readily available." Eighty-two percent
thought travel funds were unfairly distributed.

The survey item under "Professional Concerns" that
drew the strongest response was the statement, "The

budgeting process is designed to clearly inform faculty, trustees and the public." Ninety-six percent disagreed.

The level of faculty distrust of Vice President for Business Affairs Stephen Megregian in matters that ought to have been of great interest to taxpayers reflected a long history of apparent contempt on Megregian's part for the public's right to know. Irene Burnett, a past chairperson of the trustees, once told me that Megregian had stalled for months when she tried to get precise budget information. Finally, when she let him know that her patience was nearing its end, he gave the budget to her—in the form of a several-inch-thick, raw, unannotated computer print-out.

As might be expected, it was in "Part Five: Administration" that the responses were most devastating.

PART FIVE: ADMINISTRATION (POLICY-MAKING LEVEL)

(Note: This page is taken verbatim from Chapter 5, "Administrative Evaluation," in *Developing Programs for Faculty Evaluation*, Richard I. Miller, Jossey-Bass, 1975, pp. 84-88.)

The policy-making level of administration at BCC:

1. Is interested in the progress of education.

	0%	25%	50%	75%	100%	
Agree Strongly						
Agree Somewhat						+31%
Disagree Somewhat						- 70%
Disagree Strongly						

2. Instills enthusiasm for professional growth.

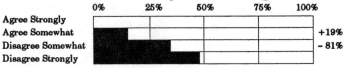

	0%	25%	50%	75%	100%
Agree Strongly					
Agree Somewhat					+19%
Disagree Somewhat					- 81%
Disagree Strongly					

3. Keeps abreast of innovations in higher education.

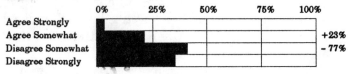

	0%	25%	50%	75%	100%
Agree Strongly					
Agree Somewhat					+23%
Disagree Somewhat					- 77%
Disagree Strongly					

4. Makes sound decisions.

	0%	25%	50%	75%	100%
Agree Strongly					
Agree Somewhat					+10%
Disagree Somewhat					- 89%
Disagree Strongly					

5. Has a sense of humor.

	0%	25%	50%	75%	100%
Agree Strongly					
Agree Somewhat					+17%
Disagree Somewhat					- 83%
Disagree Strongly					

6. Is trustworthy, honest and reliable.

	0%	25%	50%	75%	100%
Agree Strongly					
Agree Somewhat					+16%
Disagree Somewhat					- 84%
Disagree Strongly					

7. Inspires confidence.

	0%	25%	50%	75%	100%
Agree Strongly					
Agree Somewhat					+12%
Disagree Somewhat					- 88%
Disagree Strongly					

8. Maintains faculty morale.

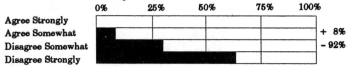

	0%	25%	50%	75%	100%
Agree Strongly					
Agree Somewhat					+ 8%
Disagree Somewhat					- 92%
Disagree Strongly					

9. Is tolerant of new ideas.

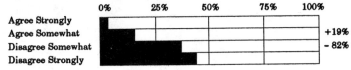

	0%	25%	50%	75%	100%
Agree Strongly					
Agree Somewhat					+19%
Disagree Somewhat					- 82%
Disagree Strongly					

10. Plans effectively and imaginatively.

	0%	25%	50%	75%	100%
Agree Strongly					
Agree Somewhat					+14%
Disagree Somewhat					- 86%
Disagree Strongly					

11. Is skilled in securing group action.

	0%	25%	50%	75%	100%
Agree Strongly					
Agree Somewhat					+19%
Disagree Somewhat					- 81%
Disagree Strongly					

12. Encourages democratic participation.

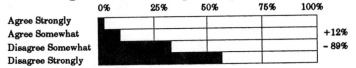

	0%	25%	50%	75%	100%
Agree Strongly					
Agree Somewhat					+12%
Disagree Somewhat					- 89%
Disagree Strongly					

13. Understands and uses modern management procedures.

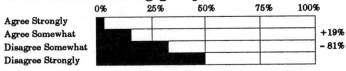

	0%	25%	50%	75%	100%
Agree Strongly					
Agree Somewhat					+11%
Disagree Somewhat					- 90%
Disagree Strongly					

14. Works effectively with faculty members.

		0%	25%	50%	75%	100%
Agree Strongly						
Agree Somewhat						+14%
Disagree Somewhat						- 86%
Disagree Strongly						

15. Works effectively with other administrators.

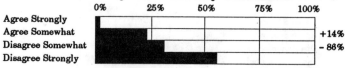

		0%	25%	50%	75%	100%
Agree Strongly						
Agree Somewhat						+25%
Disagree Somewhat						- 75%
Disagree Strongly						

16. Respects professional rights of faculty.

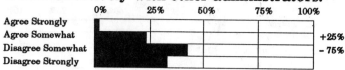

		0%	25%	50%	75%	100%
Agree Strongly						
Agree Somewhat						+19%
Disagree Somewhat						- 81%
Disagree Strongly						

17. Puts others first.

		0%	25%	50%	75%	100%
Agree Strongly						
Agree Somewhat						+12%
Disagree Somewhat						- 88%
Disagree Strongly						

18. Judges people perceptively and fairly.

		0%	25%	50%	75%	100%
Agree Strongly						
Agree Somewhat						+15%
Disagree Somewhat						- 86%
Disagree Strongly						

19. Resolves or ameliorates human conflicts.

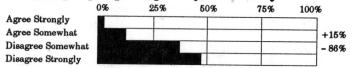

		0%	25%	50%	75%	100%
Agree Strongly						
Agree Somewhat						+17%
Disagree Somewhat						- 83%
Disagree Strongly						

20. Overall rating:

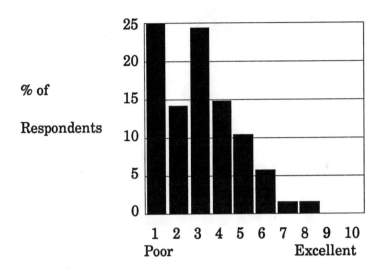

OVERALL RATING

(Exhibit #32)

In the private sector, a board of directors of a corporation the management of which elicited the kinds of responses displayed in our survey would have a new management team in place in a month.

As might be expected, faculty response in the space provided for open-ended comment required eight pages of single-spaced, very small type to reproduce. It was often vitriolic.

For example, in the section on "Physical Environment":

■ Security and maintenance are essentially ignored by the administration.

■ Facilities are designed to be high-expense in use. Technology and capital funds are not effectively evaluated and used.

■ The classrooms and offices are rarely cleaned.

(Ibid.)

In "Professional Concerns," the level of frustration became increasingly evident. Many of the responses were lengthy and detailed; others got right to the point:

■ The hiring of unqualified cronies is destroying the place.

■ Nepotism on staff.

■ Knowledge that Dr. King will not accept responsibility for these issues but will instead blame provosts, deans, or faculty.

■ Quality education is not a high priority. All show, no go.

■ I find myself shocked by my responses to this survey. Strong feelings rose as I read questions I've been ignoring, or have been afraid to respond to.

■ I feel that Dr. King considers full-time faculty as an unnecessary evil which he will reduce to a minimum as soon as possible. In NO area of his responsibility to Brevard County taxpayers do I consider his performance satisfactory.

■ It seems that Staff and Program Development funds are spent on administrators in disproportionate amounts. The professional growth of faculty doesn't seem to matter. 15% of my salary for S&PD growth equals $6,000 a year, but I'm never allowed to use even $400. Where is the rest going?

■ The recent flap over the $77,000 "awning" on the Cocoa campus demonstrates that the administration is indeed capable of detailing specific expenses in a budget the administration otherwise implies is far too complex to explain item by item. Therefore—just to clear the air—I'd like to see an itemized statement of the extent to which the Performing Arts Center is subsidized by educational tax dollars and student tuition. For example: Is the electricity bill for the Center separate from the overall operating expenses for the Melbourne Campus? How much did it cost, and who bore the expense to change the name from the Brevard Performing Arts Center to the Maxwell C. King Center for the Performing Arts? In short, does a percentage of the dollars our typical student earns at Publix and then pays for college expenses go to subsidize Brevard's wealthiest to see "Cats" or to enshrine the name of Maxwell C. King in indestructible, non-biodegradable plastic? Surely such questions are valid and relevant.

(Ibid.)

As might be expected, when survey respondents reached the space provided for open-ended comment about the administration, they had considerable momentum. Anger, despair, frustration, burnout—just about the entire range of negative emotions was reflected in the responses:

■ Encourages democratic participation? Absolute orders are hard to ignore.

■ Puts others first? In all cases of danger, yes.

■ Most major decisions involving curriculum and instruction are made by administrators with non-academic backgrounds.

■ No hope.

■ I used to blame King for draining the collegial life out of BCC, for misdirecting institutional energy, for wasting human resources, for accepting incompetence if it was clothed in loyalty, for running an ethically sleazy operation. I no longer do. He has serious identity problems, and almost certainly can't see himself or help himself, and needs professional help. I blame the trustees. Their continued refusal to better acquaint themselves with the true nature of the situation is either irresponsible or embarrassingly naive.

■ Vocational education is dying a slow and painful death at BCC due to lack of concern by the administration. Administrators have no concept of the technical expertise required in some vocational areas, nor the amount of time and effort required outside of the classroom to keep programs current and viable. Furthermore, administrators give no indication that they care one iota about the problems or that they are willing to do anything about them.

■ Dr. King holds his place at BCC not because he is an educator or even a manager, but because he has worked out a deal. His need for acceptance by the influential and the powerful leads him to ingratiate himself with them. He steers work their way, hires people they want hired, appoints them to Foundation positions, gets them nominated for trustees, etc. and they in turn protect him. Of course, he does not see it that way. He is absolutely convinced he is doing a

great job, and he cannot understand why faculty
keeps stirring up trouble . . . It is cruel to be so
blunt about this, but not as cruel as Dr. King has
been to others in his pursuit of power . . .

(Ibid.)

That the survey didn't bring the faculty to march on
the legislature and demand relief, didn't trigger an out-
pouring of citizen demand for an outside investigation,
didn't cause the trustees to call an emergency meeting of
all faculty to initiate a dialogue, would, in many parts of
America, be incomprehensible. That so serious an indictment of a high-profile social institution was received with
such equanimity would make a good point of departure
for a sociological study. I wondered if Brevard's citizens
lacked a sense of civic responsibility, or if they were
merely victims of a local media that kept them ignorant
of matters about which they ought to know.

About the only reaction to the survey that seemed
appropriate came from the editorial department of
Florida Today, and from *Orlando Sentinel* columnist
Allen Rose.

I often had fairly strong words for news staff at
Florida Today for their lack of commitment to investigative reporting. I had no similar complaints about the editorial department under Nick White. Despite what I'm
sure was enormous pressure exerted whenever the College's administration got negative press, there were
many editorials that said what needed to be said. The
only editorial I wanted to see that never appeared would
have said that King should resign. I never got a satisfactory explanation of how a leader with no followers can
lead.

On April 20, 1990 *Florida Today* editorialized:

BCC Faculty Survey Results
Demand Attention of Board

It's hard to put a good face on survey results that paint an ugly picture.

A typical defensive strategy is to criticize the critic, discount the validity of the survey and maintain business as usual.

But such a reaction may actually *exemplify* what the critics are complaining about, instead of facing issues squarely.

The dismal reflection on the administration of Brevard Community College made by the results of a recent faculty survey is too serious to brush off lightly or dismiss. Criticism of the BCC administration has been boiling to the surface with regularity during the past couple of years.

Even if the disquiet on campus has been primarily drummed up by a relatively small number of faculty members, that is not a sound reason to ignore the overwhelmingly negative opinions from 145 faculty members . . .

So, with fair questions and majority faculty participation, it would be cavalier indeed for the BCC Board of Trustees to dismiss an 88 percent low-confidence rating in its administration.

When 96 percent indicate they do not feel the process for developing the college's $35.2 million budget is designed to be clear and informative, some changes might be needed . . .

Perhaps the subjective measures given by this survey provide a more negative rating than would be drawn from other kinds of objective data. But even so, there seems to be a festering problem at BCC that will not be cured unless the board of trustees lends a sensitive ear and open mind to the thoughts and feelings of faculty members.

The faculty is "where the rubber meets the road" to carry out the basic mission of the institution. Unless a majority of the faculty members are satisfied that they can fully and freely—without fear of reprisals—address the board of trustees and get action, the atmosphere at BCC will be cloudy.

A few weeks later, on the 30th of May, the trustees would leave no doubt about how they felt about faculty having the temerity to address the board. They taught the faculty a lesson about the meaning of reprisal.

ZERO COMMUNICATION

Encouraged by *Florida Today*'s support for the idea, a meeting between the faculty and the trustees was proposed to board chairman John Henry Jones. Jones acquiesced.

We had in mind something very informal—five faculty chosen by their peers seated at a table with the five trustees. We wanted a meeting off campus, away from an institutional atmosphere. No one objected to King (or anyone else) being present, but we wanted a healthy, "real world" dialogue. We didn't think that would be possible with the trustees sitting above it all on a raised platform, behind a massive barrier, talking into microphones, with King constantly interjecting his rationalizations and "explanations."

The administration raised all kinds of objections, beginning with the tired claim that such a meeting wasn't possible because of conflict with collective bargaining statutes. We assured them that we'd be happy to steer clear of "wage and working condition" issues—the only ones about which public employees can legally bargain. We told them we just wanted to talk, and pointed

out that, after all, we were the trustees' employees just
as King was their employee. To maintain that employees
weren't allowed to talk to their employers was ludicrous.

The trustees finally agreed to the meeting, but they
balked at just about every detail of the logistics of it. It
had to be in the BCC board room. King had to be a participant. The board lawyer had to be there to be sure we
didn't get into collective bargaining issues.

All those stipulations should have told us where the
trustees were coming from. In fact, it **did** tell us that
they didn't have dialogue in mind. But we were certain
that, when it came right down to it, they would at least
want to appear to be reasonable people. If they had any
concern whatsoever about the College's problems, we told
ourselves, they'd now move beyond their standard
"Thank you for your presentation" response to faculty input at trustee meetings. Besides, there'd be lots of specta-
tors and the trustees would want to at least look as if
they were interested in institutional problems. Misgiv-
ings notwithstanding, we went ahead with plans to meet
the trustees on the 30th of May, 1990.

Once the final format became clear, no one was
anxious to participate. However, several faculty reluc-
tantly volunteered. To head off yet another one of King's
standard rationalizations that dissent at the College was
merely a union bargaining strategy, both union and non-
union members agreed to talk.

We met in the afternoon on May 30th, in an event
that is still referred to as the "May Massacre." Chairman John Henry Jones presided. Trustees Philip Nohrr,
Frank Williams, Nicholas Tsamoutales and Jennie Lesser
were also present. Future trustee Bernie Simpkins was
in the audience, his name already having been submitted
to Tallahassee for a trusteeship. His presence in the audience, my lawyers were to tell him during my hearing,
was sufficient reason in the eyes of the law for him to
recuse himself (take himself off my case by reason of

prejudice). He refused. Not only did he participate in my hearing, he chaired it.

Hindsight is great. Looking back, we realized that in the first few minutes, when untempered trustee hostility became clear, we should have walked out. The trustees had no interest whatsoever in dialogue. It was as if they had come prepared to see who could outdo whom in walking over us.

Faculty members Bob Gregrich, June England, Anna Cate Blackmon, Alan Thornquest, Dr. Neil Hamilton—each drew from personal experience in laying out major problems at the College. Each was low-key, reasonable, sincere.

It had been decided that I'd talk about those parts of the March survey that had to do with the faculty's lack of trust in, respect for, and confidence in the administration. My presentation was long, so I went last.

Aware of how delighted the administration and trustees would have been if I had said something that would have allowed them to take legal action against me, I read my presentation.

I told the trustees I was going to deal with Part V of the recently completed survey, that the section dealt with the administration, and that Part V items, averaged, gave the administration an 83.5% negative rating.

A few paragraphs into my presentation, I said:

We can't even scratch the surface of our problems in one meeting, and I don't intend to try. I'd like instead to provide what I believe to be a broad picture of how many faculty view the present situation as it relates to survey items. I'll cite cases and examples, but I don't intend them as issues to be discussed or problems to be solved. They're for illustrative purposes only. Whether or not there is hard evidence to support their validity is irrelevant. It's my understanding that we're here today not to explore what's true, but to explore faculty *perceptions* of what's true.

(Exhibit #141)

I read that last sentence very, very slowly. I'm not certain now, but I think I read it twice. I know I emphasized the word "perceptions" verbally, and I know the word was underlined in the hard copy I gave to the trustees. I don't think I could have made it any clearer that I wasn't accusing anyone of anything, merely trying to explain why the faculty felt as they did about the administration. Being a believer in the simple idea that a leader can't lead if he has no followers, I thought they ought to know why the College was, from the faculty's perspective, without leadership.

I continued:

Before I begin [describing specific problems], let me repeat that it's difficult to talk to those you don't know. If I'm too strong I may antagonize you. If I'm too circumspect you may not appreciate how serious I consider this situation to be. Please allow me a little room for error in style. I assure you that I don't intend to be abrasive, but only to reach you with what I feel are important ideas which you almost certainly don't want to hear.

Let me say also that, despite what I understand you've been led to believe, I harbor no ill will or animosity toward Dr. King. I wish him well. But I also wish the College well, and having been forced to choose between the two, I've chosen to do that which I feel is in the best interests of the College and the students. There is no "dark event" to which all my effort to bring change to this school can be traced.

Finally, let me note that, when I use the word "administration" in the following remarks, I am referring not to all administrators at the College, but only to the half-dozen or so men who bear the most responsibility for the nature of this institution.

I can't, of course, speak for anyone except myself. But here, as honestly and as comprehensively as I can state them in a few minutes' time, are what I believe to be widely held perceptions of the kind which underlie this faculty's lack of respect for and trust in BCC's administration.

I had again used the word "perceptions" to emphasize that I was merely trying to help them get inside faculty heads on these matters. In the pages that followed, each time I changed to a new topic, I began both verbally and in the hard copy by saying it was a perception.

In "Perception #1" I talked about the administration's fundamental lack of self-confidence, a lack that manifested itself in a defensive reaction to the survey rather than an attempt to learn from it.

How, I asked, would a healthy administration have reacted?

Surely it would have welcomed the survey; would, in fact, have long ago conducted the survey itself as a means of identifying problems. Instead of expressing concern for the survey responses, however, Dr. King attacks the survey. At the May 16 board meeting, he wanted to know "Who wrote those questions?" He attacks the survey. He attacks the creators of the survey. He attacks the union for participating in the survey. He even attacks the trustees for—again in his own words— "lowering" themselves to talk with us about the survey.

And when it becomes apparent that the board is going to proceed anyway, he wants to have total control of the meeting, letting stand Mr. Matheny's [attorney for the College] contention that the board can do nothing which the president has not recommended. The faculty simply asked to talk to you in an open meeting. He has done everything possible first to block us, then to allow us almost no time to speak. He has turned a meeting into a confrontation, a dialogue into a debate. We're here to explore *faculty* opinion and attitudes, and yet the administration insists on being on the agenda. Where is the logic in asking an administrator what the faculty thinks when the faculty is willing and able to speak for itself?

A healthy, self-confident administration would be here to listen. Since the subject this afternoon is not a matter about which the administration has any firsthand knowledge, I can only conclude that they wanted to be here to divert attention, to scapegoat, to minimize the available time, to pick at nits, to look for technicalities so as to subvert, to find a strategy to force the whole issue aside— here to do anything except simply listen and let others listen.

(Ibid.)

WASTED BREATH

There was more. A lot more. I talked about the administration's total preoccupation with image, talked about its lack of understanding of basic academics, talked about the crying need for classrooms and ordinary classroom furniture. I said that the faculty had heard that the administration had put the arm on Barnes and Noble, lessees of the College's bookstores, for a $30,000 contribution to the performing arts center and that it was hard to see how that money was coming from anyone except the students.

I mentioned the absence of open bidding for our lucrative humanities foreign travel program, brought up the subject of the exploitation of hourly personnel, and cited the faculty's belief—based on specific contradictory direct quotes given to *Florida Today* by Vice President for Business Affairs Steve Megregian—that the administration often dealt in half-truths or simply lied.

I pointed out the near-impossibility of getting information from the administration, information that, under "Sunshine" laws, should have been freely provided. I noted the frequent instances of faculty positions being filled by friends and family of administrators and trustees, and offered the names of people whose careers at BCC had started with bar pickups by King.

And I talked about direct and indirect intimidation, telling the trustees about student reporters who had been informed that if they wrote anything negative about the administration they might lose their student aid. I made an intentionally vague reference to an adult threatened with direct financial loss if the person should dare to write a second letter to the newspaper (vague because, as of this writing, the threat still stands, blocking that individual from testifying in my suit against the administration for fear of loss of a major business contract with an organization on whose board of directors King serves).

I concluded with a brief paragraph:

> As individuals, most of us have adapted to the
> situation. By simply disengaging ourselves, teach-
> ing our classes and going through the required
> bureaucratic motions, we can live rather comfort-
> ably with it. But this institution is dying from it,
> and doing something about it isn't one of the fac-
> ulty's options. Only you have that power. On be-
> half of this faculty, I ask you—I plead with you—to
> respect the faculty's professional judgment. Use
> your power to give us leadership we can trust and
> respect.

If I had come in carrying an assault weapon, I'd probably have gotten a more positive response. Never in my
life, not as a student, not as a day laborer, not as a truck
driver, not as a factory worker, not as a serviceman, not
as a teacher, had I ever been attacked with such venom.
I don't ordinarily lose my presence of mind, and I knew
perfectly well that I hadn't said anything for which I
could be charged, but the haranguing got to me. I walked
out.

I later learned, by listening to the audio tapes of the
meeting, that the administration had come prepared with
witnesses primed to "testify" against me. One was a retired sociology teacher whose classes had invariably been
much smaller than mine. She was considered so unreasonable by most students that many who needed sociology credit would drive to my classes in Melbourne to
avoid her. Her explanation for the great differences in
our enrollments was that I was an easy grader.

If I had known about the orchestrated attack, I might
have stayed to defend myself. Or maybe I wouldn't have.

Well, we said, so much for reasoned employer-employee dialogue. A couple of days later, *Orlando Sentinel* columnist Allen Rose gave his impressions of the meeting:

About 150 of us packed ourselves into the Brevard Community College board room in Cocoa last Wednesday and listened for several hours while faculty members and trustees recited a litany of charges and countercharges about what kind of job Max King is doing as president of that institution.

It was a sad scene for a number of reasons. Sad in that relations between Dr. King and the faculty had deteriorated to the point that a meeting involving the trustees seemed necessary at all.

Sad that it turned into more of a confrontation than a meeting of minds.

Sad that this long-festering situation could not have been resolved without a public airing of soiled linen.

A succession of faculty members stood at a microphone on the floor while the five trustees, Dr. King, and two board attorneys sat in tall, leather-covered chairs on a raised platform. And the rest of us below grew rump-weary on metal folding chairs.

I don't know who determined the format and physical setting for the meeting. But the choice clearly contributed nothing to the commencement of a much-needed healing dialogue at BCC.

This arrangement stacked the deck in favor of the administration from the outset. As the trustees looked down on the assembled mass they resembled more a tribunal chosen to pass judgment than a governing body willing to listen to the grievances of professional employees concerned for the welfare of the college.

Indeed, one speaker told trustee Frank Williams that he sounded like a prosecutor. John Henry Jones, president of the board of trustees, made it clear that he was in charge. No one was to speak out of turn. He banged his gavel when they did . . .

Trustees Nick Tsamoutales and Phil Nohrr were sharply critical of professor Marion Brady, long an outspoken critic of Dr. King, after Brady delivered a 30-minute presentation in which he accused the administration, among other things, of untruths, a disregard for the law, paranoia and exploitation of the defenseless.

"What you have said insults my intelligence," Tsamoutales said. Nohrr told Brady: "Perhaps you should look inside yourself."

Good advice. For everyone, not just Brady. All of us can benefit by looking within: you, me, Nohrr, Tsamoutales, other trustees, administrators, faculty. And Dr. King.

Differences as deep-seated as those at BCC—where some 140 faculty members have given the King administration a 90 percent negative rating in a comprehensive survey—don't occur without good reason. Rarely are they one-sided. This situation cannot be blamed on a few faculty "troublemakers," as Brady and some of his associates have been labeled.

It didn't happen overnight and it will not go away by wishing it so. Not by put-downs, confrontation, power plays, turning a deaf ear. Something is wrong and a sincere effort is needed to make it right.

The faculty met with King a couple of years ago in hopes of settling differences. They say little has changed. Hostility has continued. And most important, they contend, students have suffered. Quality education has been given lip service but has not been a priority.

In all of this, one glaring fact stands out for the trustees to consider: a clear majority of the faculty has been dissatisfied for a long time with Dr. King and his administration. That is not a *perception*.

But now the ice has been broken. Dr. King has said he would meet one-on-one with all faculty members. Let's hope these meetings are held in an atmosphere of mutual respect and that they prove helpful.

If the trustees choose to meet again with the faculty, perhaps they will do so face-to-face around a table in a sincere effort toward reconciliation.

And that they find a way to make of BCC once again the stable, respected, harmonious institution that both sides want so much for it to be.

(Orlando Sentinel, 6-4-90)

A *Florida Today* editorial said, "What might eventually do more to create a positive change in the prevailing perception of an aloof, uncaring, out-of-touch leadership is President King's announcement of a plan to hold one-on-one meetings with all 237 full-time faculty members."

As usual, however, once the heat was off, nothing happened. King met with a few people and asked them if they were happy—as if they were likely to tell him face-to-face what they really thought, knowing they'd probably be haunted by a negative response for the rest of their academic careers. He met with Alan Thornquest (another "troublemaker") and me together, and brought a couple of administrators with him.

Months later, an informal survey of about 20 teachers in "O" (for "Occupational") building on the Melbourne campus turned up only one that had had any kind of meeting with King following his promise to *Florida Today* to meet one-on-one with faculty.

TEXAS TIME OUT

In 1989, the State University of New York Press published a book of mine on curriculum theory. One of the readers of the book was Dr. Steve Mittlestet, president of Richland College in Dallas, Texas. He called me soon after the "May Massacre" and talked to me at length about the curricular innovations I had proposed in my book. A short time later, he sent two members of his faculty for a two-day visit to my classes at BCC, and came himself on the third day.

An invitation followed for me to come to Dallas before the end of the term and conduct a Friday afternoon faculty workshop. Out of the workshop came an invitation to spend a term at Richland College as a visiting professor and consultant.

After checking and double-checking the policy manual about leaves of absence, and talking with my immediate supervisor, Ann Thomas, I decided the contract negotiated between the College and the United Faculty of Florida protected me sufficiently so that I couldn't be pushed out of my job while I was gone. I applied for a leave of absence.

King's decision about whether or not to approve my application for leave must surely have been difficult. On the one hand, refusing it would be a way of punishing me. On the other hand, approving it would mean I'd be out of his hair for four blessed months. He opted for the latter, and I left for Dallas in August of 1990.

With a couple of exceptions, I didn't think much about BCC while I was at Richland. The four months proved to be a very refreshing experience. BCC and Richland had student bodies of about the same size, but from a faculty perspective the schools were very different. Richland operated with a tiny fraction of the administrative staff of BCC. I had an office of my own, with all the equipment I said I'd like to have. Faculty actually talked over lunch about intellectual issues rather than about administration-induced problems. Once a month, groups of faculty met in the late afternoon to eat and drink and discuss a current book. (Every year, a faculty committee identified six or seven books on wide-ranging subjects, put together an at-cost package of them which was bought by faculty, and each book became the focus of dialogue. My discussion group met in the president's home.)

There were other contrasts. The president's office was centrally located on the campus, directly accessible from a hallway rather than through a secretary's office. I don't remember ever seeing the door to the office closed when the president was in. Administrators regularly taught a class or two because they thought it was important to stay in touch with what the school was all about. A chair at the entrance to the cafeteria was always occupied by a faculty member or an administrator in case a student needed advice or help. There were no regularly scheduled faculty or committee meetings, but groups met often and worked hard—volunteer, ad hoc committees that disbanded when their work was done.

On two different occasions, I met a trustee of the Dallas County Community College District, both times in Richland's cafeteria. DCCCD trustees headed a system with over 100,000 students in seven community colleges ringing the city. Like BCC's trustees, they served without pay. In marked contrast, not once in 17 years did I see a BCC trustee on a campus except when a board meeting was scheduled, and they were invariably accompanied by King. When Jennie Lesser was appointed to the board, she was given a guided tour of the Melbourne campus. In advance of her visit, staff members were told that, if she asked any questions about the College, they were to say nothing negative.

I'm certain that, as is true of any organization, there were problems at Richland. But I detected no trace of the malaise, the "it's a job," the faculty-administration hostility, or the lack of trust that permeates Brevard Community College.

I can recall only two BCC-related incidents while I was in Dallas.

Near the end of my stay, I got a letter from BCC's Associate Vice-President for Human Resources Bob Lawton. He poor-mouthed about the College's financial condition, and asked that I approach the Richland administration and ask if I could stay for the rest of the school year.

I didn't know quite what to make of the request, but I suspected that, somehow or other, there was more to it than BCC's alleged financial condition. I knew that my contract with the College stipulated that a leave of absence longer than 90 work days would end the administration's commitment to return me to my previous position. At the very least, that could mean that upon my return the administration could do to me what it had done to others—send me to the campus most distant from my home, and perhaps give me a ridiculous schedule that, say, required that I be on that distant campus the last thing at night and the first thing the following morning.

My suspicions were soon verified. The evening I got home from Dallas for the Thanksgiving holidays, I got a phone call from Christine Suleski, a personal friend who had once been secretary of the arts and sciences division on the Melbourne campus. Christine had moved to the math-science department, but she maintained a close relationship with faculty from her previous position.

Ms. Suleski said she had just heard from Dr. Neil Hamilton. (Dr. Hamilton was the American History teacher who had arranged the meeting that triggered the investigation of the College's failure to pay employees for overtime work. He had also been one of the presenters at the May Massacre.) He was in Mobile, Alabama, on an unpaid leave of absence, teaching for the year at Spring Hill College, a four-year, liberal arts school.

Ms. Suleski told me that Dr. Hamilton had gotten a letter from Vice President for Human Resources Lawton telling him that his teaching position at the College had been eliminated. For reasons I'll soon point out, the administration was obviously trying to snooker him out of a job. Neil was on The List.

Unlike sabbatical leave, the kind of unpaid professional leave of absence Dr. Hamilton had been granted carried with it no guarantee of reinstatement to the position previously occupied. In the event BCC chose to eliminate a history position, however, it would have to do so by following the reduction in force (RIF) process as outlined in the College's bargaining agreement with the faculty union.

The ploy clearly was in violation of the faculty's contract. The administration eventually backed down when Dr. Hamilton threatened to hold the College to the RIF procedure, which would have required BCC to release a more recently hired history instructor at another campus.

However, when I heard about the matter from Ms. Suleski during the Thanksgiving holidays, it was still very much up in the air. She told me that a co-worker of hers had become aware of a scheme to get me to extend my unpaid leave, thereby creating a set of circumstances similar to that of Dr. Hamilton, under which BCC could eliminate my position. Without naming names, she let me know that she had learned through a credible source that this was the plan.

I told Vice-President Lawton I'd be back at the end of the term. In the spring of 1992, in a letter to the trustees reviewing my treatment at the hands of BCC's administration, I cited the incident. Lawton indignantly accused me of lying about his motives, and insisted that there was never any intention of devising a strategy to push me out of my job. How could I even think such a thing?

ANOTHER ONE BITES THE DUST

Dr. Hamilton, with whom I had stayed overnight on my way to and from Dallas, was one of many excellent teachers I had watched leave BCC. At the end of his year-long leave of absence, he decided to stay at Spring Hill College, and was made head of the history department.

I had hated to see him go. He was a tremendous asset—smart, a published book author, an enthusiastic, innovative teacher, a hard worker. More, he was willing to serve on committees, sponsor student activities and take on other responsibilities not included in his employment contract. He was the sort of person an administration that knew or cared about quality teaching wouldn't let go without a fight.

The administration not only didn't fight to keep him, they didn't lift a finger in that direction. Occasional pretty speeches by King notwithstanding, faculty quality means little to top BCC administrators. The perfect BCC faculty member is an adjunct instructor. Adjuncts are ideal because they're paid almost nothing, they receive no benefits, they have no rights, they're out of sight when they aren't in class, and they aren't eligible to join the union.

A top-level administrator who knew King well once told me that he was going to give me some useful information. "What you need to understand," he said, "is that Dr. King hates faculty. There isn't necessarily anything personal about this, he just hates them—hates them collectively—hates them as a class."

The sad thing about such an attitude, of course, was that it undermined the institution in the most fundamental sense possible. The faculty is the school. Education at its best doesn't come out of a television tube or from the pages of a book. It isn't a matter of a simple, passive information exchange; it's a highly charged emotional experience. That won't be true every day, of course, but those who've experienced good teaching are forever changed by it. Like making love or rearing children, teaching and learning are interactive processes.

Did BCC have good teachers? Of course. But it could have had many, many more. There were thousands of teachers who would have jumped at a chance to come to coastal Florida. An ad in the *Chronicle of Higher Education* would have brought job applications from everywhere.

The College had another source of superior faculty. The Brevard area had more than its share of individuals available to teach as adjuncts. A great many of them wanted nothing so much as a full-time position. They were in BCC classrooms term after term, year after year, making unparalleled observation and evaluation of their performance possible.

Were these assets exploited? Rarely. More often than not, when there was a faculty position open (and sometimes when there wasn't an opening), someone just appeared at the beginning of the term. No advertisements had been run in professional journals. No letters of application had been solicited or sent. No screening committee had been formed. No letters of reference had been received. No one had been interviewed. No visits had been

made to observe prospective teachers actually teaching.
No one had been invited to demonstrate teaching skills
in front of a BCC class. None of the procedures usually
employed to select superior teachers were routinely employed. New teachers often just showed up. No one knew
anything about them.

   Then, little by little, directly or indirectly, the story
of their appointment would emerge: This new teacher
was a friend of a business associate of King; that one was
a cousin or sister of a trustee; another was the boyfriend
of a daughter of a family friend of a high-ranking administrator.

   To the BCC administration, a faculty position was
just a job slot. If it could be used for political advantage,
it would be. If it couldn't be used to make political points,
then it was open to be granted as a favor. Particularly
appealing were those who came looking for a job with
something in their background that made them vulnerable. There were many such on campus—people who had
gotten themselves into some sort of difficulty that made
it hard for them to get a job. King loved them. Those he
hired personally he owned. He could count on them to
accept whatever he dished out.

   The BCC administration had little genuine interest in
hiring or keeping good teachers. However, even if they
had had such an interest, Hamilton didn't meet King's
definition of "good teacher." He had joined the union. He
had sponsored a student club that sometimes invited con-
troversial local people to speak at its meetings. Worst of
all, he had been a participant in the May Massacre.

   When Hamilton left, he knew that communicating
with the trustees would put him high on King's enemy
list, and that doing so would create problems should he
want to return to the College after his year's leave of
absence. However, he shared the concerns of the faculty
and wanted to do everything he could to help. Hoping
that his leaving would make a letter to the trustees more

effective because it couldn't be interpreted as self-serving, he wrote to them in June, 1990, near the end of his last term:

> At the special meeting of May 30, 1990, between the Board of Trustees and the faculty of Brevard Community College, I made a statement that "this faculty has no confidence in this administration." And I asked, "What are you going to do about it?"
>
> That comment and Dr. Maxwell King's subsequent promise to meet with each of the members of the faculty on an individual basis led to my discussing the meeting and a number of other matters with Dr. King on June 1. I will not here recite the details of the conversation, but I will convey a continued sense of great concern, even despair.
>
> The most disturbing aspect of my conversation was Dr. King's inability to see the situation at BCC for what it really is: a faculty that has overwhelmingly become alienated from the administration (and, perhaps as a result of the meeting of May 30, alienated from the Board itself), a faculty that feels shut out of the decision-making process, that feels at best secondary to the construction of new buildings, that feels victims of an attitude, real or perceived, of "throw them some crumbs."
>
> In my conversation with Dr. King I tried to stress that my comments were indicative of the feelings of most teachers at BCC and were reflective of the results of the faculty survey. Dr. King, I am afraid, sees my actions and those of others who have questioned his leadership as motivated by some personal wrong that either he or a member of the administration has inflicted on them.

This is not the case, and I, personally, am seeking no favors and no correction of an imaginary personal affront.

It is clear that faculty sentiment is as the recent survey presents it. Additionally, the sentiments of many staff members and administrators differ little if at all from those of the faculty. You do not hear from these other groups simply because they do not have the protection of tenure.

Certain individuals have, with the gratitude of most within the institution, taken on the responsibility of trying to give you a more accurate picture of reality than that obtained from Dr. King. In fact, it was the understanding of the faculty that this is what you wanted presented at the meeting of May 30. You asked the faculty to "avoid innuendo." We did, and you did not like it. The teachers came believing that they were going to be heard. Instead, most, perhaps all, of the trustees came prepared for a trial; they tried to find a scapegoat and they exhibited an unwillingness or inability to face issues. This behavior was similar to the administration itself. One can only speculate how much of this was defensive, how much of it was due to a conditioned mind-set, or how much of it was orchestrated by political colleagues. Irrespective of this, your treatment of faculty was brutal while your treatment of the administration was, by myriad accounts, obsequious.

I know well all of those teachers who spoke. Like most of the faculty at BCC they are talented and honorable people. There is not the slightest basis for believing that their sole motivation for questioning Dr. King's leadership was due to personal affronts. They are, in fact, among the hardest working and most dedicated of BCC's teachers, giving far more than their share of time and effort in committee work and other activities dedicated to improving the College. You have, in my opinion, wronged them, thereby worsening the problems. Killing the messengers will not alter the message nor will it make BCC a better place to teach.

The BCC faculty is not Dr. King's faculty, it is the community's faculty; you should not be Dr. King's board, you should be the community's board. This faculty wants to TALK to you, not debate, not argue, but talk. I hope a dialogue can still begin, but never again should this faculty be subjected to public humiliation as it was on May 30. It is much too knowledgeable and too honorable for that.

A dialogue with the faculty is important so that you can obtain a variety of views as to conditions at BCC. Dr. King's view that my action or those of other teachers is connected to something he did or did not do to me or to another individual is too constricted. I haven't the slightest doubt that Dr. King wants to do the right thing. His willingness to meet all of us individually is indicative of that. But if you begin with his skewed view of where others are "coming from," and add to that his desire to convince you that his narrow perspective is the correct one, it is clear to me that our views of what is really going on here will not be likely to coincide sufficiently for real progress to take place.

It is now your responsibility to analyze administrative procedures at BCC in full. It is Dr. King's responsibility to come to grips with the implications of the survey results. It can only be hoped that your efforts, his efforts, and the efforts of the faculty will coincide so as to produce a positive, favorable atmosphere of education at BCC.

My question, "What are you going to do about it?" remains quite pertinent and awaits a reply.

(Exhibit #34)

Years later, the trustees still hadn't talked to the faculty, hadn't shown any inclination at all to move beyond King's narrow perspective on reality to explore faculty anger and alienation. For his part, King still hadn't met one-on-one with the faculty, hadn't come to grips with the meaning of the survey.

I suspected that would never happen.

Hamilton talked about King's assumption that opposition to him could be traced to some personal affront. This peculiar idea appeared over and over in the President's discussion of problems at the College. In his mind, it appeared, everything was personal. I felt that this personalizing of all experience lay at the heart of his success and his failure. His legendary fund-raising achievements in Tallahassee, his ability to weave some sort of cocoon around every trustee, his growing wealth through outside business ties, the apparently blind loyalty he inspired in a few of his associates—all could to a considerable degree be attributed to an effectiveness in one-on-one, paternalistic relationships. His tendency to see every situation as a product of favors or affronts was probably a facet of this.

But the favors and affronts that seemed to loom so large in King's mind were of little consequence to most individuals who chose academic careers. They were more interested in principles and policies, ideas and fields of study. They weren't looking for a father figure who'd pat them on the head if they were good; they wanted a system supportive of quality instruction. In a better job market, faculty turnover at BCC would almost certainly have been horrendous.

ZERO COMMUNICATION. STILL

I think it was in February of 1991 that several members of the faculty union attended a dinner for Brevard's legislative delegation. The affair took place in the Foundation House, a motel-like structure in the far northwest corner of BCC's Cocoa campus.

The evening was unremarkable. The food was standard, the speeches predictable, the exchanged compliments proper. I waited for an opportune time to leave gracefully. Unfortunately, I was sitting at the table farthest from the exit, making an inconspicuous departure impossible, especially if I had been the first to go.

But I wasn't the first. As those who attended BCC trustee meetings knew, Trustee John Henry Jones wasn't one to wait around to see how things turned out. For him, elsewhere often called before a meeting chairman's call for adjournment.

True to form, while the affair was still in progress, Jones excused himself and left. To my vast surprise however, he got up from his table near the exit, walked around the end of all the other tables in the room, came to me, shook my hand and said something amounting to "Have a good evening."

Only those who knew how much weight King put on such matters could have appreciated Jones's action. In King's eyes, even the most casual fraternization with the enemy was unacceptable. Now, Jones had singled me out of the whole crowd and, in front of everyone, appeared to be markedly friendly. Surely, I thought, this was significant.

I had said to several people that, at the May Massacre, Jones was the only trustee whose behavior was reasonably temperate. I had also been told by a couple of ex-public officials—Roger Dobson and Dixie Sansom—that Jones wasn't solidly in King's pocket.

Significant events often have insignificant begin-
nings. Always looking for a way to get a foot in the door,
I thought Jones might offer possibilities. Maybe I could
work with him in a positive way. His handshake was a
small gesture. However, added to the other information
I had about him, cooperation seemed at least a possibility. I decided to write him a conciliatory letter suggesting
that we put the past behind us and focus on positive
steps to improve the situation.

On March 1, 1991, I mailed him a letter:

John Henry, I appreciated your willingness to
greet me civilly the other night. Some of the administrators can hardly bring themselves to do so.

Well, the May meeting is behind us. It's a
temptation to discuss subsequent events in matters about which I was called a liar and threatened with legal action, but I'll bite my tongue.
[e.g. The federal investigation verifying my charges of Wage and Hour Law violations.]

The meeting is over, but it seems to me we're
about where we were. I haven't the slightest
doubt that the situation will continue to deterio-
rate, but I do think there are positive actions
which could be taken to slow the deterioration.
One of those actions (as I've told Dr. King) is to
follow the lead of colleges like Dade and radically
decentralize. Even healthy institutions function
better when that's done, and in this case it would
have the additional benefit of distancing the central administration from those who no longer
trust or respect it. There would be problems at
first, as the campuses got used to having real
rights and responsibilities, but giving each campus formula-based funding and then getting out of
the way could do much to push the source of

anger and frustration—the central administration—
into the background.

(Exhibit #146)

I continued in this same tone, making seven more
proposals that I felt might help get the College on a positive course:

2. Clarify budget categories.
3. Add a democratically elected, non-voting member of the faculty to the board of trustees to
   improve communication.
4. Adopt a firm policy that all faculty positions
   would be filled via a screening committee.
5. Clarify the role of line administrators. (Are
   they supposed to be educators or managers?)
6. Move the ratio of administrators to teachers
   closer to the national average.
7. Set up a system for evaluating administrators.
8. Reconsider meeting informally with faculty, or
   at least stopping by the College occasionally
   when not in King's tow.

(Ibid.)

Each of the proposals was elaborated and explained.
I then concluded with a plea that he look beyond secondhand information about me and get in closer touch:

I know the word "pariah" is attached to me.
I also know that years of administrative effort to
discredit me have succeeded with the trustees and
some of the faculty. If, in any of the five other

institutions in which I have worked I had been perceived as a troublemaker, if the results of the faculty survey had been any less clear, if my contacts with community leaders led me to think I was out of bounds, I might think there was some justification for the administration's attitude toward me. But none of those are the case.

So, I'll continue to work with other faculty to try to get this institution to fit the image its press releases attempt to convey. Having no real power, about all we can do is make noise. Most of the faculty is too tired and frustrated to do even that, but some of us haven't quite given up hope that we can make a difference. Until we do, we'll probably get louder and louder.

Of course, all this is damaging to the College. But I'll stake my self-respect on the contention that there's nothing we can do to make our situation public which equals the long-term damage being done by this administration. Maybe, just maybe, it will eventually get through that it will take something more substantial than presidential chats with faculty to reverse the debilitating apathy, anger and frustration which robs this faculty of so much of its potential.

(Ibid.)

I attached to the letter a small chart that I felt underscored the educational ground we had lost in the preceding ten years:

NUMBER	1980	NOW	% CHANGE
STUDENTS	10,934	14,226	+30%
FACULTY	230	228	- 1%
LIBRARIANS	9	7	-22%
COUNSELORS	13	5	-62%

(Ibid.)

I had made a sincere effort to be constructive in order to get some sort of dialogue going. In less than a week I had a reply. It was signed "John Henry Jones." However, I told several people that, if he actually wrote it, I'd eat the computer disk he put it on.

Dear Mr. Brady:

I was astonished by your most recent letter. You open by referring to the May meeting of last year. At that meeting, the contrast between your rumors, charges, and inaccuracies and the administration's reliance on facts gave us a clear understanding of who was the source of anger and frustration. It wasn't the administration as you alleged then and allege again in your letter. The source was and is you. Your tactics were described by two Trustees as resembling McCarthyism.

I have noticed another significant contrast. The administration is constantly working to make this college better. Their success has been recognized not only locally, but also by their peers on a national level. It seems to me that the objective evidence suggests we truly have one of the nation's best community colleges. By my observance, it seems the harder they try to build the college in an honest way, you try to tear it down using any method you think may work.

I think it's a disgrace that you have on a regular basis compiled lists of rumors which largely consist of clear untruths and then solicited them to everyone possible. When a given list is shown to be not substantiated by fact, you start all over by releasing a new list of rumors. One of the Trustees last May 30, after observing your frightening display, remarked that you seem to have some kind of obsession. In your latest letter, you state of the effect of your future acts, "Of course, all this is damaging to the college."

There is a very precious right of free speech in this nation, but there is also a responsibility not to shout "Fire!" in a theatre when there is not a fire. I seriously suggest to you to follow the union contract provisions on Academic Freedom and Correlative Obligations (Article 17). It states, "When a faculty member writes or speaks he/she must recognize the special position in the community he/she holds as an employee of Brevard Community College in that the public may judge both the faculty member's institution and profession by his/her statements. Therefore, the faculty member shall at all times strive to be accurate, to exercise appropriate restraint, to show respect for the opinions of others . . ." The administration has the responsibility to follow that contract. You do, too. They have the responsibility to continue to build our college, not tear it down. So do you.

You have the responsibility to do the best possible job teaching. The administration has the responsibility to do the best possible job running the college. Please concentrate your comments to me if you wish to contact me again on how you can become a better teacher. For example, would it help you be a better teacher if you could earn your Ph.D.? If so, let us know how we can help you do this. Do you need classroom equipment? Is your teaching load too much or too little?

Mr. Brady, it seems as though you have a greater interest in becoming an administrator than in teaching. If that is so, have you ever checked into obtaining additional education and training and seeking employment in this area?

In the face of specifics from objective observers who are peers, your continuous inaccuracies are especially offensive and repulsive to those of us who value the truth. As I read your latest communication, I noted that at least you are consistent. On the last page where you show a copy of a paid ad you are considering, you include another inaccuracy. You state, "with a second planetarium underway." There is no second planetarium. Plans are for the present one to be expanded, not a new one built. You should have known this. Dr. King invited you and the others on the union executive board to the legislative dinner this year where this was clearly explained. The President thought he could try to ease your negative feelings by inviting you. I guess he was wrong.

(Exhibit #147)

King was so pleased with the letter that he had it sent to the other trustees, to all administrators, to selected faculty, to members of Brevard's legislative delegation and even to key people in Tallahassee. Most of them got their copies before I got the original.

Jones was obviously a lost cause as far as the faculty was concerned, but I could at least attempt to defend myself to those to whom his letter had been sent. I wrote him in March:

Your letter, to understate my feelings considerably, was a disappointment. I had come out of the May meeting with an impression that you were, on the whole, even-handed, objective, professional, and aware that the situation called for some fresh thinking. With that impression in mind I wrote you, suggesting, in good faith, eight positive ideas, ideas which have worked in other institutions with problems similar to ours.

Obviously you weren't interested in talking about possible solutions. You dealt with my letter in the same way the trustees dealt with the May meeting. Both were approached not with any intent to listen and explore ways of working constructively together on our problems, but as opportunities to attack, to berate, to belittle, to divert attention, to find a scapegoat.

Your response to my memo allows me to continue holding my original impression of you only if I believe you didn't write it. You did, however, sign it, so I must assume that you agree with its tone and content, and that you approved of its being broadly distributed to my fellow faculty members, to all administrators, and to state officials in Tallahassee. I am left wondering, however, why dozens of copies were released before I received the original, why some copies were sent to faculty anonymously, why the original letter came from the president's office, why it wasn't sent to my return address at home, and most importantly, what you hoped to accomplish by refusing to respond to a single one of my suggestions, choosing instead to attack me personally. Was it merely another in a long history of administrative attempts to intimidate? Was it just a put-down? Was its shrillness meant to convince the legislators and the public, once and for all, that if it weren't for Marion Brady, BCC would be a big, happy family?

I suppose this last was the real motive, for hardly a week goes by that the message isn't repeated by someone in the administration. How the trustees can believe that I have the ability to convince 83.5% of faculty to suspend their own judgment and give this administration a negative rating is beyond understanding. College teachers are as varied a lot as you're likely to find in one place, they all have advanced degrees, they're all adults, and they were all smart enough to be hired here. It's absolutely ridiculous to think that they'd let me make up their minds for them.

That 83.5% figure is, by far, the single most important fact in this entire situation, and the trustees steadfastly refuse to deal with it. Even if it were true that this administration is so far ahead that mere faculty can't catch the vision, even if we were entirely wrong, even if the president really were a "semi-God" as the student newspaper portrayed him, don't we still have that most serious of institutional problems—a crisis of leadership? Explain to me, please: How can a leader be effective when only 16.5% of his followers are with him?

Leadership in this situation isn't possible, of course. All we're proving right now is that, with a reasonably good faculty, a college can function without a leader.

Could you also explain to me what is accomplished by attacking ME? What have I done? Let me tell you. I've deleted the profanity and said out loud what most of the faculty has been saying since long before I came here. Nothing more.

You began your letter by contrasting my "rumors, charges, and inaccuracies" with the administration's "reliance on facts." Without plodding once more through every issue raised at the May meeting, allow me to recall the primary one, the one which, if I remember correctly, elicited the McCarthyism charges against me. I said that the administration had for many years been illegally exploiting wage and hour employees by requiring that they work far in excess of forty hours a week while pretending that they were part-time employees so as to avoid paying them benefits. I wasn't there later in the meeting, but I understand that, in reference to this matter, Mr. Megregian added "liar" or some such similar word to the McCarthy label attached to me.

Could you explain to me, please: If what I said was a "rumor, a false charge, inaccurate"—if I am a liar—why in the world did the college subsequently agree to write $18,000 worth of checks to employees for back wages? (And would have paid out far more if all accounts with employees had been squared in cash.) Are you saying my ability to influence others to do what they would not otherwise have done extends even to the Wages and Hours Division of the National Labor Relations Board? Are you saying that the college didn't really owe the money but paid it anyway? Mr. Jones, what, exactly, IS your definition of the word "fact" when you insist that this administration deals in them?

(Exhibit #187)

I went on to discuss Mr. Jones' offer to "help make me a better teacher," responded to his speculation that what I really wanted was to be an administrator, and concluded:

Finally, am I, as you suggest, "obsessed"? I'm more inclined to view my activity as an interesting, educational project, a project having the virtue of reflecting the concerns and helping to contain the fears of a large number of people I like. When so many people have been so unhappy for so long, for such inexcusable reasons, somebody needs to try to hang in there long enough to do something about it. I am committed to the improvement of the college, but I will decide for myself how best to do that. Surely, SURELY, I am by any measure better qualified than ANY of my critics to make such decisions.

Does the situation warrant determined effort to bring about change? Absolutely! Forget, if you choose, every rumor. **If I knew nothing whatsoever about this school except (a) what is printed in the annual reports, and (b) the percentage of faculty who have said they no longer trust the leadership, I would know that you are standing watch over a pretty corpse propped up by public relations.**

In the interest of fairness, I respectfully request that all those to whom your letter was

copied, directly, indirectly and anonymously, be
given a copy of my response.
Thank you.

(Ibid.)

SACS "EVALUATION"

In what was originally intended as a way to maintain
and improve educational standards, school accreditation
was developed. In the southeastern part of the United
States, the official accrediting agency is the Southern
Association of Colleges and Schools (SACS).

Every ten years, institutions wishing to maintain
their official accredited status are supposed to spend a
year scrutinizing themselves using guidelines developed
by SACS. The self-study completed, they then host a
visiting team of "experts" drawn from other institutions
who come in, look around, ask questions, and write reports pointing out what they consider to be institutional
strengths and weaknesses.

In theory, it's a good idea. SACS guidelines reflect an
awareness of the kinds of problems endemic to schools,
and are designed to require self-study activities that
encourage reform. In practice, however, there are many
ways to maintain the status quo while making it look
like SACS guidelines are being followed.

The simplest way to avoid real change—the way other
faculty told me BCC did it in 1971, and the way I know
from firsthand experience that they did it in 1981—was to
form all the necessary self-study committees, have them
meet and come to their conclusions, write up committee
reports identifying problems and inadequacies, and send
them to an administrator/editor. This "editor" then
rewrote them to make them fit the College's public relations image. A few minor problems were usually admit-

ted to make the report believable, but according to the edited versions of the report, BCC's "forward-looking administration" was well aware of the minor problems and had them all but solved.

If a SACS visitation team didn't share the administration's view of the situation, that didn't pose a threat. By the time the visiting team's final draft came back, long after the investigators left, nobody looked at it. The media was no longer interested, and most teachers were too busy or too cynical about the whole procedure to care one way or the other.

As the visitation for the '90s approached, we were determined that the '70's and '80's procedures wouldn't be repeated.

We wrote a letter to SACS telling them about BCC's history of subverting the evaluation process. SACS didn't answer. We decided we'd attempt to meet with team members off campus at their hotel. We couldn't find out where they were saying.

The team came and left. A few of its members seemed aware of and sympathetic to our problems, but the comments of the team's leader, the president of a community college in Virginia, left little doubt that the whole evaluation procedure was largely a sham. In a final effort to push the SACS report in the direction of honesty and candor, on the 14th of February 1993 we wrote a letter to SACS' Executive Director, Dr. B.E. Childers in Decatur, Georgia.

The Southern Association of Secondary Schools and Colleges' Visitation Team has just left town.

Twenty years ago and ten years ago, Brevard Community College's SACS institutional self-studies were widely perceived by the faculty as gross distortions of the true state of affairs at the College. When the reports were released, the fac-

ulty realized that it had been outsmarted, that the
College's administration had edited the reports
and omitted all but the most superficial criticisms
of the College.

The words of SACS team captain Dr. S.A. Burnette at the opening banquet and during the exit
presentation suggest that a third whitewash may
now be in progress. In the two previous distortions
of reality, the faculty blamed the administration's
duplicity (and its own naivete). This time, it appears that SACS itself is a party to the coverup.

There followed single-paragraph summaries of familiar problems. The paragraphs noted that three faculty
surveys, including one just completed for SACS, gave the
administration disapproval ratings of between 83 and
96%; SACS team members had themselves noted that a
"pervasive fear" seemed to mark the College; entire academic fields had been abolished to facilitate the firing of
particular teachers; documentation had been given committee members regarding serious problems in the BCC
Foundation.

, The letter included a summary of an incident witnessed directly by the SACS Team—the arrest of ex-BCC
counselor Alan Thornquest and student Andrew Spilos
for demonstrating in front of the King Center for the Performing Arts:

Team members watched three police cars
arrive to break up a very small, absolutely peace-
ful demonstration asking that SACS not be a
party to another whitewash. Surely the irony
could not have escaped college professors. They
witnessed this gross violation of First Amendment
rights—rights they, of all people, should hold

dear—from a private, members-only liquor lounge (a lounge built at public expense, in a public building, on public property). The demonstration resulted in two arrests "because it was not held in a designated protest zone"—a parking lot out of sight and hearing of the SACS team . . .

What prompts this letter is what came across as a parting slap in the faculty's face. The SACS written report, yet to be received, may indeed note many of the problems of this institution. But no matter its content, it will not negate the impact of Dr. Burnette's words in the Thursday morning exit presentation. He said, "Anyone who takes anything said by this committee to mean anything else other than this is a fine institution has misinterpreted the work of the committee. Anyone who might attempt to use anything said or written by this committee to reflect negatively on . . . this institution will be doing both this Committee and this institution an injustice."

Perhaps there was no prior "arrangement" between the two community college presidents. Perhaps there is no truth to the rumor that Dr. King's brother is a community college president in the same system as Dr. Burnette. Perhaps there is an acceptable explanation for the difficulties BCC's faculty had in its attempt to learn the names and local accommodations of the visiting committee so that it could try to arrange to meet with them privately. Perhaps the visiting committee was unaffected by the wining, dining, and "hovering" of the College administrators during their visit. Perhaps Dr. Burnette's words were not deliberately meant for "damage control" from team members at least some of whom seemed to interpret the situation less positively than did he.

We concluded with some words about the long-term consequences for SACS' credibility when evaluations were rigged, and stapled a copy of *Orlando Sentinel* writer Allen Rose's February 6, 1992 column to the letter:

This one's for Bud. I have said for months during the Brevard school fuss over possible loss of accreditation by the Southern Association of Colleges and Schools that it doesn't really matter what happens.

SACS is a meaningless bunch of academic stuffed shirts whose time has passed. And whose accreditation is an empty sack.

All of which was confirmed this week when a SACS evaluation team got themselves a junket to Florida to visit Max King's personal fiefdom, aka Brevard Community College.

Team captain S.A. "Bud" (as in good ole boy) Burnette, president of something called the J. Sargeant Reynolds Community College in Richmond, Virginia, left this parting shot when he left town Thursday: "Anyone who takes anything said by this committee to mean anything other than this is a fine institution has misinterpreted the work of the committee."

Well, Mr. Bud, I hope you will not misinterpret this: The mission of Brevard At Large is opinion and commentary. And you are about to get a generous helping of both.

Anyone who has stayed abreast of Max King and his autocratic administration has to know that BCC has the *potential* to be a fine school. Perhaps it will be when Max finally hits the road and takes along the toadies with whom he surrounds himself.

Under King, those who toil at BCC do not enjoy freedom of speech or dissent guaranteed to all
Americans. A prime example: trumped-up charges
against professor Marion Brady, and the kangaroo
court hearings on whether Brady should be fired.
Brady's chief accuser was a dean whose academic
credentials, revealed last week, were highly ques-
tionable, to say the least.

Another was the arrest last week of former
BCC counselor Alan Thornquest and a former student for demonstrating outside the college during
the SACS visit. They failed to move to a parking
lot where they could be seen by virtually no one
except the night watchman. Thornquest, another
King critic, was fired last year in what King
called a faculty reorganization.

So, Mr. Bud, be assured we will not misinterpret your report. We accept it for what it is: a pile
of paper worth about 25 cents a hundred pounds
at the Yorke-Doliner junk yard in Cocoa.

SACS' Dr. Childers said it wasn't appropriate for him
to respond because of my legal situation. He didn't
explain why that had anything to do with the SACS
team's behavior, neither did he explain how he even
knew about my legal situation.

PJC 'EPIC' trips questioned in auditor fund examination

BY OBIE CRAIN
Special Projects Writer
Pensacola Press Gazette

Pensacola Junior College's (PJC) affiliation with a "travel-related" organization known as EPIC (Educational Partners for ...

AUDITS OF THE college for years mentioned tell of thousand dollars in membership fees, ". . . approximately $5,000 for trav the President, one other employee a Board member for EPIC-related

HCC's costly community spirit

Tampa Tribune

Hillsborough Community College has spent thousands of dollars on gourmet meals, private club membership, and tickets to dances, receptions and other social events for President Andreas Paloumpis and his top administrators.

HCC officials say the expenses are a necessary part of "networking," making contact with local business and community leaders.

But the expenditures also reveal much about the school's priorities. Is networking *this* important? Cocktail conversations, after all, do not lead to academic excel

The profits of HCC machine and cafeteria Activity Fund, whic public-relations a 1972 sanctioned special funds.

Students' d money paid in writers Jim Slo only $9,000 (during the pa students.

HCC spokes out that many co social events whil used for scholarsh

to Manatee Community College, w president personally pays for his t banquets and other functions. Or HCC to St. Petersburg Junior Colle spent but $13,000 last year on publi and hospitality events.

HCC officials emphasize that HC of Trustees want the school more i the community. Showing the col thing. But is it worth spending $60,000 on socializing? What be derived from, say, Paloumpis and ding the Mee oumpis a g to a Ast en sa c

Audit critical of community college

By BARBARA BEHRENDT
St. Petersburg Times

CRYSTAL RIVER — State auditors have critici way Central Florida Community College (CFCC with its booster club and the way the college property records, credit card transactions and grants.

BCC's wall of secrecy ds up costing us all

3½ emphatic pages, the 4th istrict Court of Appeal has dered the Palm Beach nity College Foundation to stop public records from the public.

Dr. Eissey's mission of deception eats money that could have been

Report: DBCC picked Xepapas in 'flawed selection process'

Daytona Beach News-Journal
DAYTONA BEACH — Daytona Beach Community College chose architect Andy Xepapas as developer for its troubled Deltona area project through a "flawed selection process," according to a preliminary audit report released Monday by state Auditor Ge

The report also concluded that DBCC failed to obtain the required bonding from Xepapas, financed the project in a way not authorized by state law, and violated the terms of its contract by erroneously paying Xepapas his $200,000 profit before ground was even broken for the pro-

FCCJ foundation spending criticized

By Joan Hennessy
Staff Writer
Florida Times-Union

Trustees of the Florida Community College at Jacksonville questioned the accounting policies of the college's private fundraising foundation after learning yesterday it had paid about $12,000 in travel expenses for the FCCJ president and his wife for a three-year span.

the public document Eissey's mission

Part IV

THE HATCHET MAN

I returned to BCC's Melbourne campus in the fall of 1991. Over the summer, King—in yet another move reflecting his unhappiness with Dean Thomas and Provost Flom for what he saw as their inability to quell the open opposition to him by Melbourne's faculty—transferred them to Cocoa. Their Cocoa counterparts, Provosts Robert Aitken and Dean Stevan McCrory, were assigned to Melbourne.

Aitken wasn't happy. He had been at BCC for many years, knew how King's mind worked, and had made the necessary compromises to survive. He had begun his career at BCC as a baseball coach, and had moved slowly up the ranks of BCC's administrative hierarchy. He liked to be liked, and was adept at convincing those he was with that he had their best interests at heart and would do what he could for them.

And he did, as long as their best interests were such as not to come to King's disapproving notice.

The primary reason for Aitken's unhappiness with his assignment to Melbourne was McCrory. Aitken and I knew each other well, and talked often over breakfast or sitting in his car. He had stories to tell—lots of them—about McCrory's performance the previous year in Cocoa.

I don't know the circumstances surrounding McCrory's hiring by King. Perhaps it was just another of many politically expedient moves, or perhaps it helped the College meet mandated racial quotas. Maybe he recognized McCrory's hatchet man potential from the very beginning.

Whatever the reason for McCrory's hiring, it certainly had nothing to do with a striving for academic excellence.

Max & Me

He was a recently retired Air Force sergeant. He had no background in academic administration. His transcript suggested that much of his college credits came from correspondence courses. Even so, his grade average wasn't the sort one associated with leadership of a college academic department. And, when it came to advanced degrees, McCrory's paperwork suggested several different stories from which one could choose.

No one I talked with on the Cocoa campus considered McCrory's performance as anything other than appalling. In a matter of weeks he had the Cocoa liberal arts department in turmoil. McCrory knew little or nothing about how the College functioned, but that didn't stop him from issuing orders, military style, about what was to be done. Faculty schedules that had been in place for years were arbitrarily changed with extremely confusing results. Some teachers found themselves scheduled to teach two different classes in two different rooms at the same time. Others discovered that they were assigned classrooms already occupied. One teacher was assigned double the usual number of classes.

When problems stemming from his orders were brought to McCrory's attention, he reacted in ways alien to higher education governance. In one case, several teachers asked Henry Carrier, a faculty member with long service, to talk to McCrory about their confused schedules. Carrier did, but got nowhere. Turning to leave McCrory's office, he asked what he should tell those who were waiting to hear what could be done about schedules in disarray. McCrory didn't hesitate. "Tell 'em," he told Carrier, "that I said, 'fuck 'em'."

He made major changes in the department. The division secretary was no longer the division secretary; she was his private secretary. The photocopier was moved out of the faculty mail room and into his office area, and the secretary—a young girl—was put in charge of telling experienced faculty what they could and couldn't copy. Saying that he wanted to teach everybody a lesson about leaving musical instruments in unlocked lockers, McCrory took saxophones home with him without telling anyone in the music department.

Hardly a day passed that McCrory didn't do something to anger or frustrate those he supervised.

In the spring of 1991, I began to hear a rumor from several different members of the Cocoa faculty. The source of the rumor, I was told, was long-time faculty member Mary Cathryne Park. She knew King well, and I figured she knew what she was talking about. (Later, when I confronted her, she denied having said anything.) The story was that McCrory was going to be reassigned to the Melbourne campus to assert administrative authority over the rebellious Melbourne faculty, and that he had a "special mission" to "get Marion Brady."

I didn't think much about it. I assumed that, when push came to shove and it came to a public hearing, there'd be a reluctance on the part of the trustees to openly ignore fairness and decency. I'd been at the college for 15 or 16 years. I had tenure. I'd been on just about every College committee of consequence. I'd voluntarily assumed responsibility for tasks not required by my contract. I'd worked hard. My performance reviews were above average. (Not great, but above average. Before coming to BCC I'd always been rated an outstanding teacher. I considered my BCC evaluations quite an accomplishment considering the pressure on my supervisors to find something negative the administration could exploit.) I hadn't attacked any co-eds, hadn't "borrowed" any College property, hadn't parked on the grass, and had solid support from a great many faculty whom I admired for their strength of character.

And I'd learned to laugh at most of the administration's juvenile, heavy-handed attempts to harass me— strategies such as ordering BCC's librarians (verbally, of course) that they weren't to help me with any research.

So what could they do to me?

I had had no personal contact with "hatchet man" McCrory when the term began. Even in early September, when the Melbourne liberal arts faculty got together in a special, impromptu meeting to review some of McCrory's actions and discuss what to do about him, I could only listen.

What the faculty decided to do was to meet again two days later, call McCrory's boss, Provost Bob Aitken in, and ask what he intended to do about McCrory's behavior.

The second meeting took place, and Aitken got an earful. One faculty member told of walking away from a three-sided conversation involving McCrory and a student and hearing McCrory refer to him as "that asshole" to the student. Another told of submitting a proposal related to an honors program to McCrory, a proposal she'd been working on for months, and being told that BCC didn't need "any of that crap." Just to be sure she understood, he called her proposal "bull shit." A third described having classes that had agreed-upon enrollment ceilings being vastly overloaded. She protested, and McCrory came to her class while it was in session, pulled her out, and was hostile and abusive to her in front of students.

And so it went around the room. The common thread in nearly all the testimony was that McCrory's behavior was so off the wall and unprofessional that nobody even wanted to talk to him.

Aitken was clear and unequivocal. We didn't have to put up with that kind of treatment, he said. And if in the course of any meeting with McCrory **anything** happened that we considered unacceptable, we could stop the meeting and insist that it be continued in his (Aitken's) office.

I had had no confrontation with McCrory when the liberal arts faculty first met with Aitken in the fall of 1991, but it wasn't long in coming.

I GET VISITS

In most organizations, taking action against an employee requires the building of some sort of file to document problems. Since much of what happens in a classroom is open to a variety of interpretations, even the best teacher is at risk in front of a class. I've spent a great deal of time supervising and teaching teachers. I think I could observe just about anyone and put together a plausible-sounding, truthful, devastating critique of what, in fact, was an acceptable performance. Teaching is a complex process, judgments about it are subjective, and those who do it are always somewhat vulnerable.

For this reason, I felt that classroom visits by administrators represented a hazard for me. Early in the fall of 1991, Tace Crouse, new Provost of the Cocoa campus, had spent a week on the Melbourne campus. My class was the only one she visited. Later, when I brought that fact to her attention, she attempted to cover herself with a couple of belated notes to other teachers saying that she had observed them from the hallways outside their classrooms. The fact remained that, out of about 70 teachers, I was the only one on campus into whose classroom she came. I was obviously a marked man.

For years, standard procedure at BCC was for faculty to be observed once a year. In fact, many teachers were never visited by administrators, including some on the Cocoa campus who were under McCrory for the entire previous year. I assumed, then, that when McCrory came into my class he was on a fishing expedition. When he came in a second time a short while later, he removed any lingering doubt I might have had. The administration's strategy—at least part of it—was clear. The year had barely gotten underway and the process of attempting to stuff my personnel file had begun.

The increasing pressure notwithstanding, I remained confident that I could survive any attempt to do me in. It having been more than six months since I had published a guest column in *Florida Today* (their maximum frequency), I used my reeligibility to continue to try to bring what I felt to be important issues to public attention. About the middle of November, I submitted a guest column called "How To Shut Me Up" to the editors. They toned down the title to, "**If they change college operations, there'll be no more rabble-rousers,**" and published it on the 25th of November, 1991.

Those who follow Brevard Community College in the pages of *Florida Today* may know that I'm not very popular with most of the college's upper-level administrators. Over the years, they've made that clear. In-house bulletins attack me. Anonymous letters question my character. Supervisors pay "friendly" visits to my classes. Attempts are made to de-certify me. Stuff I write gets sent to a high-priced south Florida lawyer (at taxpayer expense) to see if action can be taken against me.

Because I know what a source of frustration and embarrassment I've been to the college's administration, I'd like to suggest a ten-step strategy for shutting me up:

1. Adopt a budget which shows the full cost of each ancillary activity—Performing Arts Center, Village Playhouse, planetarium, television station, golf driving range, Indian festival, etc. If we're broke, it would surely be useful to know what it's costing taxpayers for facilities, salaries, maintenance, equipment, advertising, insurance, public relations, printing, postage, utilities and security for non-educational activity.

2. Open broad, threat-free channels of communication between trustees and faculty and staff—

particularly to secretaries, security personnel and maintenance workers. (Ignorance may be bliss, but it's a poor basis for policymaking.)

3. Organize like every other college in the country: with department heads. Surely it isn't unreasonable to want, say, a social science department headed by someone who knows something about social science.

4. Hire on merit. Period.

5. Observe the letter and spirit of Florida's Public Records Act.

6. Dump the command-and-control management style. (I sure wouldn't want my kids being taught by teachers willing to shuffle to paternalism or salute authority.)

7. Cut the public relations budget by about 80%. If we're doing great things, the word will get out.

8. Stop trying to intimidate those who question the status quo. And stop scapegoating. The basic problem isn't me, the union, the lower-level administrators, or "a few disgruntled faculty." Take responsibility. I see by the computer printout that my bosses are the only administrators who don't get raises. I'll bet the explanation they've been given goes something like, "if you were a **good** administrator, you'd know how to handle Marion Brady." Take responsibility.

9. Cut the bureaucracy. Radically. Nationwide, the ratio of "executives, administrators and managers" to teachers in community colleges is 1 to 11.45. At BCC, the chief-to-Indian ratio (based on titles in the new phone book) is 1 to 3.1.

10. Get interested in education. In 1980, BCC had 10,000+ students and 230 full-time teachers. Now, we have 15,000+ students and 232 teachers. In 1980 we had two libraries and nine librarians.

Now, we have four libraries and six librarians. In 1980, we had thirteen counselors. Now, we have three.

I hereby publicly affirm that, if the college's administrators make a sincere effort in these directions, or satisfactorily explain why they should not, I will have one of the lowest profiles in the institution. I much prefer teaching to rabble-rousing.

STUDENT "COMPLAINTS"

McCrory's next move wasn't long in coming. I was called into his office and handed some handwritten documents.

In the course of teaching thousands of students at four high schools, three colleges and two universities, never once, as far as I know, had a single student written a "report" to an administrator about my activity in class. McCrory now handed me two such documents. No names were on them, so I assumed that they were turned in anonymously. I recognized the handwriting of one of them as that of a student in one of my classes. The paper said that in the student's sociology class, I had discussed the administration of the College. "Mr. Brady," it said, "believes he is being targeted by the school's administration, because of his strong opinions against the running of the school. Reasons:"

1) Feels the school is run now like a business and not very much interested in conveying knowledge.

2) The ratio of teachers to students is worse now than ten years ago.

3) The King Center is a waste of money. Feels the money should have been put into the tools of education.

4) Feels there are a few good teachers, but on the whole more bad than good.

5) Commented on how old some of the tools of education are. Talked about holes in walls, old falling apart desks, old carpeting. He said these are examples of an administration that does not care.

(Exhibit #61)

The second paper made the same points in a slightly different format and style.

I'd never considered it appropriate to spend class time on matters not related to the subject at hand, so my first reaction was that the incident the students described had never happened. Then I remembered my *Florida Today* guest column, and recalled that, on the day it appeared, an older, newspaper-reading student had asked about it before the start of class. Other non-newspaper-reading students, hearing our discussion, asked about the column. I summarized it. The whole discussion, according to students with whom I subsequently checked, didn't run into class time more than a very few minutes. And if it had, they said, what of it? Part of what sociology is all about is the study of the uses and abuses of power.

I wrote to Provost Aitken about the matter:

The morning of December 20th, I was called by Mr. McCrory's secretary and told that Mr. McCrory wanted to see me in his office about a "student matter."

I went to Mr. McCrory's office. He handed me photocopies of two documents which he said had been given to him by students. No names were on the documents. They were in the form of reports of statements I had allegedly made in a class on November 12, statements critical of various matters related to the college. (Copies are attached.)

I read the documents, and told Mr. McCrory that I considered them trash.

I have difficulty believing that the documents came into being other than at the request or encouragement of Mr. McCrory or someone else in the administration. I contend that:

1. Students do not voluntarily submit these kinds of documents to deans. On those rare occasions when students go directly to administrators with a faculty-related matter, they do so out of long-term anger or frustration with a classroom problem not otherwise resolvable. In neither of these documents is there a hint of anger, or even of dissatisfaction. What would have been the motive for writing them?

2. The documents are in the form of reports. Why, other than in response to a request for information, would such a style be used? That they are alike in this respect strains credibility.

3. On two occasions last term—once in a day class and once in a night class, in response to direct questions from students who had read a reference to me in the newspaper, I cited the views expressed in my guest column in *Florida Today*. My responses were very brief, and I terminated the conversation with the statement that such dialogue was an inappropriate use of valuable class time. Even if the two documents were in the form of complaints—which they were not—the complaints would have been unjustified.

4. The documents allege that I expressed opinions **which I do not now hold and have never held.** I have never expressed anything even close to the opinion that a college should be run like a business. I do not believe that, and I did not say it. (I have said, on other occasions, that school administrators should note that hospital administrators do not dictate operating room procedures.)

5. The documents contend that I said BCC had only a few good teachers. This is the statement which prompted my comment that they were trash. (Actually, I think the word I used was "crap.") This amateurish attempt to drive a wedge between me and the rest of the faculty is preposterous. Even if I thought such a thing—which I certainly do not—I would never say it. I *have* said, repeatedly and in the presence of *many* witnesses, that in my experience the college had *more* than its share of outstanding faculty, and that it was sad that the administration here was such that they could not realize more of their potential.

That suddenly, after forty years in the classroom, TWO written documents would be handed to an administrator, UNSOLICITED, SPONTANEOUSLY, SIMULTANEOUSLY, MAKING IDENTICAL FALSE STATEMENTS, is far beyond the bounds of the believable.

What explanation could there be other than that the documents were solicited? What is the point of them? Why did the students not say something if they were interested enough in my opinions to write them down on the spot? (As my students will testify, I encourage disagreement and dialogue.) Why did not Mr. McCrory respond as most administrators would have responded, asking the students if they had talked to me? Since the reports show no evidence of anger, why are they anonymous? Why, given the administration's supposedly strong stand against anonymous documents, was something made of these?

(Exhibit #162)

I had my own theories about the papers. I already knew from faculty lounge gossip that one of the two students spent a great deal of time—sometimes as much as an hour and a half a day—in McCrory's office with the door closed. The kind of relationship suggested by that amount of personal contact prompted conclusions otherwise not plausible.

I heard nothing from the administration about further action against me related to the reports. A few days later I left for the Christmas holidays, and thought no more about them.

Several weeks later, Melissa Prevatt, a fellow faculty member, told me she had been approached by a student asking for advice about what to tell a friend who had been approached by McCrory and asked to submit written material about me. The student didn't feel the query was in order, but was reluctant not to cooperate with a College official.

I had a vague, fleeting memory that years before, faculty member Bill Wenz had been hauled up for an administrative hearing based on "complaints" from students. The students were never identified.

STUFFING THE FILE

Hatchet man McCrory tightened his grip on the axe handle. The details are too tedious to recount, but administrative strategies in which he played a role came down primarily to two.

Brevard Community College faculty are required to spend 35 hours per week on campus. Ten of those hours are for "student advisement"—hours when teachers are in their offices and available to talk with students.

As those familiar with my schedule were later to testify under oath, I spent a great deal of time at the school. Like most faculty, however, although I generally observed office hours, I didn't go to great pains to be physically inside my office door every minute.

There was little reason to be there at all. For months at a time no one would come by. Those students who had questions invariably stayed after class rather than make a special trip. Those who wanted to talk about grades or other private matters either called me at home or made other arrangements. Like many teachers, I didn't have a private office, and students were understandably reluctant to discuss their grades or personal problems in front of strangers.

Generally, I used student advisement hours to study or grade papers. But, like everybody else, I felt free to go to the bathroom, get a drink, pick up my mail, go to the soft drink machine, or run other short errands. If I thought I'd be gone for more than a few minutes, I'd either tell my office mate where I could be found or leave a note on the door.

For 16 years, this was acceptable. In fact, for several of those years my office enclosure was six feet away from my supervisor's office door, putting my leaving and returning in plain view. Nothing was ever said.

Writing me up for "neglect of duty" was therefore a cinch. A 16-year habit is hard to break. McCrory would catch me picking up my mail or returning from the cafeteria and put another reprimand in my file. Even though I knew what was happening, the whole thing was so bizarre I couldn't seem to take it seriously.

The second issue between us had to do with his continuing visits to my classroom. When I confronted him about his motives, he insisted that he had made multiple visits to other teachers. When I pressed him for names, he told me "Pat Jones." I checked. Yes, she said, he had been to her room twice. He came the second time at her request. She wanted him to feel for himself the classroom's excessively high temperature.

The harassment was so blatant that I began to get pretty hostile. To a sergeant type, of course, any kind of open antagonism or questioning of authority is unacceptable. He wanted respect and I'd damn well better give it to him.

If my job hadn't been on the line, much of this would have been pretty funny. McCrory observing and taking notes about me. Faculty members Jeff Neill, Pat Jones and others observing and taking notes about McCrory observing me. Comic opera.

One specific incident became the focus of much subsequent administrative action, and was much of the basis for the final trustee action against me. McCrory had ordered me, by way of his secretary, to come to his office. Knowing that I would again be treated like an infantry recruit, I recalled Provost Aitken's words in our impromptu faculty meeting. I told the secretary to tell McCrory that I'd meet with him, but I wanted Aitken to be present.

She forwarded the message, and he called me back himself.

"You will meet with me," he said, "and Aitken won't be present."

"I'll meet with you, but only if Aitken's there."

"You will meet with me, and Aitken won't be there!"

After about the fourth exchange in identical language, I hung up. This incident was the basis for about half the charge against me of insubordination. (The other half came several months later, when he was no longer my dean but was still ordering me around. I gave him a snappy Nazi salute.)

On January 27, 1992, I wrote McCrory a long memo summarizing our relationship up to that date.

From that memo:

> To review the basis for the charge of gross insubordination: It is true that I "failed to comply with a clear and reasonable directive . . . to attend a scheduled meeting." As I explained to you prior to that meeting, however, I considered your intent in scheduling it hostile and, consistent with my understanding of information from the Provost, I asked that he be present. A few hours later, after learning from him that I should have at least put in an appearance, I came to your office, apologized, and offered to talk. You informed me that you had nothing to say. I interpret that as evidence that your real intent had nothing to do with a substantive issue, but that you were merely seeking a basis for lodging a charge against me.

> If I had not taken you at your word that the Letter of Reprimand would be withdrawn [a reference to another incident], I would have grieved it immediately, charging that your initial unprovoked hostility toward me, your unreasonable refusal to honor my request that the provost be present at our meeting, your unwillingness to accept my subsequent apology, your refusal to handle minor matters by simply picking up the telephone and talking them over in the manner of professionals, and your charging me with gross insubordination, were ample evidence of an intent to harass.

On January 16, I was handed a second Letter
of Reprimand. It charged that I "grossly misrepresented the facts" in a letter to the Melbourne
Provost, that I "violated proper chain of command
by not first discussing" my concerns with you,
and that my language and expressed intent to
grieve your action was unprofessional.

I reject those contentions. To review the issues:

With the exception of the very first meeting, I
have shown up at your office at every scheduled
time. Our discussions about a textbook, about
your visits to my classes, and about the two
anonymous letters from students have been brief,
but discussions there have been. I therefore violated no chain of command. I simply took the next
step. I wrote the Provost because your abrupt and
frequent orders that I come to your office, your
discourteous failure to indicate the reasons for the
summonses or the agendas of such meetings, the
hostility implied by your repeated advice that I
bring witnesses with me, your invariable calling
in of a second administrator, convince me that
these are no ordinary meetings on ordinary
matters. In a "normal" work situation, such
trivial matters would be settled in brief conversations in the hallway or on the telephone.

Concerning the most recent incident involving
the anonymous documents purportedly written by
students:

It is a basic right, reflected in the policy manual, that the accused be permitted to face accusers. The school term in which this action occurred is past, and the grades are in. Reprisal—
even if I were so inclined—is not possible. As I
have previously noted, the documents merely allege that I discussed college affairs in class and do
not indicate that the students objected. I therefore

have no reason to feel antagonistic toward them. Before your second letter is placed in my file, bring the students forward. Because their actions have implications for my reputation and my livelihood, I believe it would be appropriate that my counsel be present.

(Exhibit #157)

There followed more discussion reviewing the relationship between McCrory and me. I ended on a general note:

It is common knowledge that the highest ranking administrators at the college have repeatedly said that a way needed to be found to get me out of the picture. Some of them have told me so themselves. I stand firmly on my contention that you are cooperating with them to that end, and that your strategy is to turn matters of little or no significance into bases for disciplinary action. Perhaps more important than their impact on me, your actions have seriously demoralized the liberal arts department. I consider such methods thoroughly unprincipled, and will use every means at my disposal to create an institution where the concept of professionalism has an ethically-defensible meaning.

(Ibid.)

WHO'S IN CHARGE HERE?

On the 15th of February, I was called in to McCrory's office to go over his evaluation of me for the previous (1991) school year. It was, of course, by far the worst evaluation of my career. Word for word and letter for letter (I'll forgo the use of "sic,"), here's McCrory's summation:

Comment on items marked "BE" [Below Expectation]: #6: During this evaluation period, the documentation Mr. Brady submitted to me were all subjective, unprofessional, and misrepresented the facts. On at least one occasion, I had to send a follow-up memo requesting the information. #7: In almost all situations, Mr. Brady initiates and responds to both oral and written communication in an unacceptable destructive, unprofessional manner. #8a: Mr. Brady has no respect for his immediate supervisor or administrators above him. He consistantly bypasses his chain-of-command in an effort to stymie the productivity of the organization and seems to strive on brining about conflict. #10a: A review of Mr. Brady's syllabus raises numerous questions as to where his course is going. The required textbook for the course is not used throughout the term, grading on "Gordon Rule" assignments are ambiguous. **Recommended Professional Development:** Mr. Brady needs to focus on developing a more professional image by following the rules of the college. More important, he needs to cease his efforts of being destructive. Mr. Brady needs to understand and follow his administrative chain-of-command when questioning policy, practices, and procedures. To assist and enhance the learning process, I strongly recommend that Mr. Brady used the required textbook throughout the semester. Finally, I encourage Mr. Brady to develop a course syllabus prior to the beginning of the semester, so that students clearly understand the direction of the course.

(Exhibit #69)

I refused to sign the evaluation, responded in writing to all the charges, and filed one of many grievances. It was all, of course, a waste of time. The final decision on all grievances rested with the administration, and I had by this time learned that, when it came to the administrative chain of command, McCrory didn't have one. He worked directly with King.

That there was a direct relationship between McCrory and King was obvious. In April 1992, *Update* carried a front- page article entitled "Who Is In Charge Here?"

On Tuesday afternoon, April 14, nineteen members of the faculty of Brevard Community College, Melbourne Campus, converged upon the office of the Provost to inquire about Mr. Stevan McCrory, former dean of Liberal Arts and Business. Even though the Board of Trustees formally voted to "eliminate" the dean positions on March 13, and even though the faculty was told March 5 that the changes were to be effective "immediately," Mr. McCrory continues to call himself the Dean and continues specifically trying to harass and intimidate sociology Professor Marion Brady.

On the morning of April 12, with only five minute notice, Mr. McCrory "observed" Prof. Brady's teaching for the **fourth** time in three months. In a follow-up conference, Prof. Brady was faulted for "jingling his pocket change" and putting his foot on a chair. Mr. McCrory challenged Prof. Brady's presentation on "static and dynamic aspects of societies," asking how that was relevant to a class in American history. And since Mr. McCrory said he was unable to make the connection for himself, he told Prof. Brady that he intended to continue to observe his subsequent classes, looking for an answer.

At the confrontation with the Provost, the faculty asked for an explanation. The Provost tried to be reasonable and told the faculty to be patient with the "transition," to wait it out, and not to worry. He assured them that he personally was in complete control and would take care of it. When he was specifically asked if that meant that he was the one who ordered Mr. McCrory to harass Prof. Brady, however, he said simply, "No."

The only conclusion left to the faculty is that while the Provost is claiming complete authority for the Melbourne campus, he has no control over Mr. McCrory who, evidently either takes his orders from no one and is the proverbial loose cannon—or takes his orders directly and only from Dr. King and is Max's ax man.

Meanwhile, Dr. King professes not to understand why faculty morale is less than it might be.

Latest update: On Monday, April 17, just three days after the faculty protest to the provost, Mr. McCrory again observed Prof. Brady. There can no longer be any doubt: Dr. King has made it clear that he holds the faculty and their educational goals in complete contempt.

(Exhibit #39)

At the meeting referred to in the *Update* article, Provost Aitken was asked the same question at least three times: "Have you ordered McCrory to harass Brady?" Three times, in front of 19 witnesses, he answered "No."

I stayed in Aitken's conference room until the others left. He again repeated that McCrory was out of his control. In fact, he said, he thought McCrory was trying to do both of us in. He then told me that, a few days earlier, when he and I had briefly gone off campus to a bank together, within 15 minutes of our return he had gotten a "casual" call from King wanting to know if he and I "ever go off campus together." Aitken was certain that McCrory had called King in an effort to get him in trouble.

A few months later, during the hearing leading to my dismissal, Aitken said under oath that the 19 faculty who heard him say that he wasn't responsible for McCrory's harassment of me had all "misunderstood."

What put all of these events in peculiar perspective was the fact that, weeks earlier, on March 5, the faculty on all three campuses had been called together simultaneously to hear an announcement that, in an administrative reorganization, all dean positions excepting that of Allied Health on the Cocoa campus were being immediately abolished. Faculty member Julia Brooks, with McCrory's behavior clearly in mind, asked the question on the minds of the entire liberal arts faculty: "Did you say this reorganization is effective immediately?" The firm response from Aitken? "Yes, immediately."

Ah, I thought, I'm off the hook. In a chronology I had started keeping, I wrote "NO MORE McCRORY" in big letters across the page for that afternoon.

And that's what everyone else thought, which explained the anger in the meeting with Aitken. We had already been told, in the clearest of language, that McCrory was no longer a dean. Why, then, was he continuing to stuff my file?

The explanation seemed apparent to the faculty. In the decision to abolish the dean positions, McCrory's "special mission" was forgotten by the administration. Then, realizing that McCrory hadn't finished with me, a lame attempt was made to claim that he hadn't been included in the reorganization. A phony memo was even fabricated supporting the administration's contention. When it surfaced during my hearing, I pointed out that the memo referred to events that hadn't yet taken place on the date the memo was supposedly written, and that it had a distinctive format used only by Director of Employee Relations Bob Craig rather than by Aitken's secretary, from whom the memo had supposedly come. The College's attorney said nothing more about it.

A final bit of evidence of the administration's determination to make me hold still while McCrory beat up on me: In March, I attempted to put some distance between McCrory and myself by applying for a transfer to Cocoa. I noted in my memo that there were at least three openings in Cocoa, that I had originally come to Melbourne at Bob Aitken's personal request, that the Cocoa campus was much nearer my home, and that the tripling of the number of traffic lights in the eight or nine years I'd been driving between Cocoa and Melbourne made the commute a waste of valuable time.

My seniority would ordinarily have meant that the transfer was routine. However, instead of a transfer, I got silence. When, six weeks later, I pushed for an answer, I got a sarcastic response from Vice President Lawton with no word about my requested transfer.

The administration continued to stall. When I finally got a response to my request for transfer to Cocoa, my experience and my seniority netted me instead a schedule from hell: morning and night classes at Palm Bay; morning and night classes at Melbourne, the two campuses farthest from my home. The time spread between classes meant that I'd rarely see my house in daylight. I couldn't even use the time for useful work. Palm Bay's library was totally inadequate.

The administration, of course, had an explanation. They said that Palm Bay needed experienced teachers. When I pointed out that Edison Feu, my office mate, was an experienced teacher, was willing to teach at Palm Bay, and lived about five minutes from the Palm Bay campus rather than nearly 40 miles away, there was no response.

From dialogue at board meetings, it was clear trustees thought the College's grievance procedure was adequate for dealing with problems such as this. In fact, it was all but worthless. More often than not, the grievances were against the very people who decided whether or not the grievances were valid. In any case, the ultimate decision rested, for all practical purposes, with King. Even if the procedure worked, it took so long that it was useless for matters such as arbitrary schedule changes and transfers. By the time the process had run its course, the changes would have long since been in place.

LAST STRAW

By March it was clear that the administration was pursuing custom-built strategies for those on its hit list. Tom Ward, the only other full-time sociology teacher, had

152   *Max & Me*

learned that, without even consulting the sociology teachers, the administration had removed sociology as a
required subject for the nursing program. The obvious
plan—a much-used one by the King administration—was
to cut program enrollments, then point to the low enrollments as a reason to abolish the program. To get to me,
they had to get rid of Tom. (Over the years, a long list of
faculty had been forced out by abolishing programs. At
the time, the administration was also using it to get rid
of the horticulture teacher, Craig Edwards. Edwards'
students and private citizens vehemently protested the
abolition of one of the College's most promising vocational programs, but the administration stalled until the pro-
testers got tired, then finished the program off after the
trustees had forgotten about it.)

Tom and I attended the March meeting of the board.
Since the trustees routinely passed every King proposal
unanimously, the meetings were invariably dull. This
time however, Linda Parrish, president of the faculty
union, had been invited to speak. Although she had been
asked to limit her remarks to "something positive,"
Linda had a mind of her own. We thought she'd say what
she thought needed to be said whether or not the trustees
would define it as positive, and we were curious about
trustee reaction.

In fact, there was considerably more dialogue than
usual, and in the course of it trustee Jones said that he'd
heard lots of rumors about harassment and intimidation,
but that he'd never seen any evidence of it. He'd like
some examples.

Linda's office was near mine. The next day, I asked
her if she thought it appropriate for me to respond to
Jones's request. She couldn't see any reason why not, so
I began to put together a review of experiences I felt at
the time were meant to harass and intimidate me. In a
memo to the trustees dated March 31, 1992, I listed 22
incidents. I then took one of the incidents—events subse-

quent to my contacting the National Labor Relations Board about BCC violations of the Fair Labor Standards Act—and discussed it in detail, adding information I was pretty certain would be new to the trustees about how the College "solved" the payment of reparations to employees by not allowing them to work until the College had recouped its money.

I reminded the trustees of their own harassment of the faculty during the "May Massacre," and of their own harassment of me when my recounting of the College's role in the underpayment of employees led them to threaten me with legal action. I noted that:

> No trustee ever apologized to me for wrongly accusing me of lying. No one even said, "You were right." Perhaps most importantly, no trustee asked (at least out loud) if there was something wrong with a system that shielded them from important information which could perhaps have brought considerable trouble to the trustees themselves.

> *(Exhibit #116)*

A few paragraphs later:

> Surely all this suggests questions: Why should I rather than the trustees know about matters of such importance? Why should I rather than the trustees be given detailed documents alleging large scale felonious activity at the college, documents complete with names, dates, subjects and amounts? Why should I rather than the trustees be told about equipment costing hundreds of thou-

sands of dollars, purchased, milked of its public
relations value and now inadequately maintained
and unused? Why should I rather than the trustees receive anonymous lists in the mail of dozens
of relatives, friends and political cronies hired at
the college without appropriate competitive procedures? Why should I rather than the trustees be
approached with information about the college's
secretive behavior in relation to the planetarium?
Why should I rather than the trustees know of
situations which threaten to lead to serious suits
against the college at a time when the college can
ill afford such suits?

Why do I not pass along this information to
the trustees? Read again how I was treated by the
trustees when I tried to minimize institutional
damage by working quietly and behind the scenes.

I ask again the same question I have been asking for years: Is it not just possible that a couple
of hundred faculty members—adults, people with
advanced degrees, people many of whom have
taught at other institutions of higher learning,
others who have been here for decades, people
supposedly selected because they stood above their
peers in ability and intellect, people who know the
details of the programs only the glittering summaries of which reach the trustees, people who work
day in and day out at the college, people who
would disagree on any other subject you could
bring up—is it not just possible that when they say
they neither trust nor respect this administration,
their collective judgment may deserve more
respect than the trustees seem willing to give it?

(Ibid.)

I concluded with the matter of my transfer to the Palm Bay campus:

> Week before last I was informed that the administration planned to send me to the Palm Bay campus next fall.
>
> I live miles north of Cocoa. To reach Palm Bay I will have to pass the Cocoa campus where, in the fall, at least three and possibly four full-time positions in my fields will be open. To reach Palm Bay I will also have to pass the Melbourne campus where, in the fall, at least three more full-time positions will be open.
>
> One more fact: Edison Feu, an experienced teacher who is qualified in the same fields as I, lives in Palm Bay, just a few minutes from the campus, and has said he would like to teach at Palm Bay.
>
> Now tell me. In your view, is the intent to send me more than 35 miles, past two campuses with at least six full-time positions open in my field—is that deliberate harassment or is it not?
>
> As I have repeatedly said, I am not by nature a confrontive person. And I certainly would much prefer spending these very moments on matters directly rather than indirectly related to the quality of education we can offer students. But someone needs to speak up when taxpayers are being bilked, unprotected people are being exploited, students and teachers are being threatened, and the individuals, agencies and media who **should** be aware of the problems and doing something about them close their eyes and refuse to assume responsibility.

(Ibid.)

For Dr. King, the letter was the last straw. He began to make plans for the next meeting of the trustees.

And McCrory continued with his special mission. He observed my class on April 17. At the conclusion of the class, Jeff Neill and Pat Jones, faculty who had come to observe McCrory observing me, stood with me near the door talking. Students for the next class—not one of mine—began filtering in. One of them, a girl I couldn't recall ever having seen before, excused herself for interrupting and asked if I was Mr. Brady. She introduced herself as Elaine Fowler. Student friends of hers, she said, had been approached and asked if they'd be willing to write negative reports about me.

I could hardly believe the amateurishness constantly displayed by the administration in its pursuit of me. Every move was transparent. Surely, I thought, nobody could take these people seriously. I didn't adequately appreciate that finesse wasn't necessary. All the administration needed was an excuse to get me up in front of the trustees. From that point on, the desired outcome was assured.

Part V

THE SET-UP

As usual, Dr. King prepared a strategy for the April meeting of the trustees that ignored the message and attacked the messenger. With a vengeance. The plan was to invite me to the meeting, then tear me limb from limb.

I knew the routine. I'd been there before. So I wrote a note to Frank Williams, the only trustee I knew personally, and gave it to union president Linda Parrish to give to Frank before the meeting started:

Late yesterday afternoon, Dr. Aitken informed me that my March 31 memo to the trustees would be discussed at the next board meeting, and that I had been invited to attend.

It was not clear who had invited me, or if I was expected to speak to matters related to the [March 31] memo. In any case, I will not be attending, and would not have wished to speak if I had attended. I have steadfastly maintained that the board meeting format constitutes a hostile environment for faculty within which effective communication is all but impossible, my one appearance before the board was nothing if not unpleasant and unproductive, and my impression is that the board sees itself as an arm of the administration. Those reasons combine to assure me that my non-attendance is appropriate.

I will be happy to answer, in writing, any questions relating to my experience at the College. If the trustees have a genuine interest in the matter my memo addressed—harassment and at-

tempted intimidation of faculty and students by
the College's administration in attempted denial
of First Amendment rights—a study by individuals
having no connection with the College would seem
to me more helpful. (Perhaps Roger Dobson and
Irene Burnett might be willing to play such a
role. One is Republican, the other Democrat; both
have chaired the trustees; both have buildings
named after them; both should be perceived by
the trustees as, if anything, predisposed toward
the trustee perspective.)

(Plaintiffs' Exhibit #191)

The constancy and the volume of the administration's
attacks on me, and King's perhaps genuine righteous in-
dignation at all the "damage" I caused and the money I
was costing the taxpayers for investigating my claims,
sometimes led me to wonder if maybe I really was out of
touch with reality. Whenever this happened, I'd suggest
something like the above—the calling in of a neutral
party—an outside consultant, a survey firm, an independent hearing officer. King's steadfast refusal to allow
objective analysis of the situation was always very reas-
suring. If I was willing to listen to disinterested parties
and he wasn't, I had the assurance I needed of my own
mental stability.

The board meeting was in Titusville, and Linda was
a few minutes late. Not wanting to walk up front during
board proceedings, she waited until the so-called "Citizen's Presentation" period and then handed my memo to
the board's secretary.

The memo was clearly addressed to Frank Williams.
However, instead of giving it to Frank, the secretary
gave the original and all copies to King. He, in turn,

gave a copy to board attorney Matheny. Linda doesn't recall whether or not copies were given to other trustees.

According to my lawyers, this April 7 board meeting was, for all kinds of reasons, extremely important. It was their view that, even if the trustees had come to the board meeting with no prior knowledge of me or the situation, the meeting itself and a package of materials King mailed to the trustees the next day would have so compromised their objectivity in the eyes of the law that they could not possibly have heard my case without bias.

And that's only if they had come to the meeting with no prior knowledge, which certainly wasn't the case for any one of them. All had been exposed to King's continuing on-the-record diatribes about me. It's hard to imagine that he hadn't been even more vocal in his private communications with them. As I noted earlier, Simpkins had been present in the audience at the "May Massacre," had, in fact, already been appointed a trustee of the College. Not only did he refuse to recuse himself from hearing my case, he actually served as chairperson of the three-trustee panel.

Some random quotes taken directly from audio tapes of the April 7 meeting provide a feel for its tone:

KING: . . . And then when the board got a most recent letter from Mr. Brady, I felt in talking with my administrators that we should use this board meeting to let my administrators, who are responsible in this area, to respond to the board and somehow or another we have got to get some sense into some of these people who, when, we're working so hard to have a positive image about the college in the legislature and have these people in the house trying to tear it down. It just doesn't make any good rational sense to me . . .

We've smiled and turned our cheek for three years to this sort of thing. And I think it's time, and I think the board should know it's costing taxpayers' money and resources when we have to research all these wild ideas that certain people come up with . . .

The thing that's frustrating, Mr. Chairman, to members of the administration and, frankly, members of the public, that this stuff is distributed to everybody and his uncle is they don't know the difference between what is true frustration and what is a lie. And there are some lies in that letter. That's the point that I'm frustrated about.

(Exhibit #50)

About a dozen pages of the transcript were taken up with procedural questions about what kinds of actions the trustees could and couldn't engage in when dealing with employees. In the course of the discussion, Frank Williams said that if my actions were "damaging to the college and university, if that continued slander and whatever it is is damaging, may we not sue him?"

Healy then raised a question:

HEALY: Mr. Chairman, I think—I whole-heartedly agree with our counsel that it would be inappropriate for us to sit up here and deliberate issues that are appropriately addressed through grievance procedure. But in this particular instance, I think we have to be mindful of the fact that we solicited this letter.

When Ms. Parrish was speaking to us at the last meeting, she was trying to explain why many members of the faculty felt they didn't have appropriate access to the board of trustees, that the only access they had was at the meeting, and many of them felt that they were suffering from intimidation that prevented them from coming and addressing this board.

And we asked—I don't know if it was me—but I specifically recall one of the board members asking her if there were examples of that, they should be brought before the board. And this letter is a response to that request that we made.

So the purpose of this letter really, it could be viewed not as Dr. Brady saying I have these grievances and I want the board to address this, these specific grievances; it could be viewed as you wanted to know why I don't feel free to simply come before the board and express my opinions about the way the campus is operated, is because I feel intimidated. And why do I feel intimidated, is because of these specific events that I outlined in this letter.

(Ibid.)

Healy had it exactly right, but Simpkins and Moehle obviously weren't interested in derailing a procedure designed to get me that had already been set in motion.

SIMPKINS: I don't think our comments solicited this kind of response.

I believe we encouraged faculty, or the union, to come before the board with things that were positive [!] and things that would help us posture a better education. I don't think we solicited anything like this . . .

MOEHLE: I don't think that this was an adequate response to anything we solicited either. He did not appear here to make his plea so that he could be asked questions.

He wrote a letter and refused to come to be available for any questions we might have of him personally concerning his allegations. So I don't think it was a proper response at all.

And I do think—I agree with you, Bernie—but I do think that something does need to be done about the fact that a letter like this is not so much a complaint to the board of trustees as it is a vehicle for, as Dr. King said, sending the letter all over the world, to everybody and his brother to stir up more controversy.

(Ibid.)

SPRING THE TRAP

In the course of the dialogue, Board Attorney Matheny had made it clear that if the trustees listened to BCC administrators making negative statements about me, their ability to sit as an unbiased hearing body would, in the eyes of the law, be compromised. That I had been vilified by the administration in any number of earlier trustee meetings appeared to be forgotten. With the end in sight, it was now time to give the proceedings at least a superficial appearance of legality.

So King backed off. He wouldn't have McCrory, Craig and Lawton give their presentations, not orally, anyway:

KING: If you don't want to hear it, we have written responses . . . and I will give them to the board, put them in the mail tomorrow, if you

choose not to hear them today. And you'll have
written responses to every one of those allegations. And you'll find in it that there's a number
of untruths in the comments. Further, I have his
immediate supervisor here to tell you, that as far
as he was concerned, after his observation and so
forth, he had recommended dismissal. But because
of various legal interpretations, we've not gone
beyond his recommendations. But all that's in
writing and I'll give it to you tomorrow.

(Ibid.)

Healy had displayed a bit of reasonableness and independence. Jones did the same. He said he was concerned
about violations of the First Amendment:

JONES: I think we should be extremely careful in attempting to deny this gentleman the right
to speak . . . I've heard that on many occasions in
the past that what this gentleman says is untrue,
yet I failed to see any lawsuits on behalf of this
college for slander or anything of that type . . . I'd
like to know why some legal action hasn't been
taken if these statements are untrue.

(Ibid.)

Jones then raised a question about the College's violations of the Fair Labor Standards Act to which I had
referred in my letter.

This wasn't a matter that King and at least some of
the other trustees wanted to talk about:

WILLIAMS: We need to decide the issue of whether we're going to follow Mr. Matheny's advice or not before we get the answer to that.

JONES: I have the right to ask the question, don't I?

KING: If you remember—you may not remember, the board had a report on this, on the wage and hour study, and that was given to the board some time ago. To distinguish is wrong, you're wrong. But there's a half-truth to that.

JONES: Was there any amount paid?

WILLIAMS: I just think that we're getting into—

JONES: You're denying me my right to ask the question, Mr. Chairman, and I resent that very much.

KING: No money was paid, Mr. Jones. It was not—it was not entitled to the individual. [According to *Florida Today*, about $18,000 in back wages was paid.]

WILLIAMS: Mr. Jones, I'm sorry, I would let the attorney decide whether or not that was a proper question. We haven't decided whether we will take this issue up or not.

JONES: I'm on this board, Mr. Chairman, I intend to ask questions as long as I sit on this board with or without the attorney's advice or consent or what have you. The day comes that I can't ask a question, I'll get the hell off the board.

(Ibid.)

This was a refreshing departure from the usual trustee dialogue. It continued for a total of 38 pages. If there was anything that came through loudly and clearly, it was that King had decided to put me on trial, Simpkins knew it, and he didn't want any of the board's proceedings on this occasion to block that course of action. Time and again Simpkins came back to the subject, even when it didn't follow from the preceding dialogue:

> KING: But we've got answers to all this. This refutes it [the "charges" in my letter]. You know, it will be charged. It's not Dr. Brady, it's Mr. Brady. He doesn't have a doctor's degree. He'll say this is board-administered intimidation. But I wanted you to hear his supervisor, who doesn't think he's a good teacher. And we've said, you know, he's a great teacher.
>
> But his supervisor is the only one been in the classroom talking to him about that. But I can get that to you in writing. And we'll just let it go from there.
>
> SIMPKINS: Mr. Chairman, and I'd like to pose a question to our general counsel, if we hear that today, does that prejudice us from sitting as a judicial body at some future time?
>
> MATHENY: There is some risk of that.
>
> SIMPKINS: That's my concern.

> *(Ibid.)*

On the 5th of May, I wrote to all the trustees:

> I don't understand. At the March board meeting, I clearly heard the trustees ask for information about administrative harassment. The minutes of the meeting verify that such a request was made.

I responded in good faith. What did I think would happen next? Since this is a college, within a society with a professed commitment to logic, reasonableness, fairness and the rule of law, I thought I would be asked to document what I had said.

Instead, according to Ms. Parrish's notes, Dr. King responded to my letter by saying it contained "wild ideas," "lies," and "wild and untrue allegations," and at least some trustees appeared to accept his statements as settling the matter. One said, "If this slander continues, can we sue him . . .?"

Under the circumstances, given the board's close working relationship with Dr. King and its willingness to make judgments about me based on second- or third-hand information, I would expect a bias toward his perspective. But am I wrong or exceedingly naive to think that the above kind of talk is premature? If I've lied, appropriate action should be taken against me. I would expect it. (I don't buy Mr. Matheny's contention that I can get away with it because Dr. King is a public official.) But is it too much to ask that you **investigate** and **then** make up your minds as to who is lying?

Perhaps it's now expecting too much to ask for neutrality and objectivity. That matters have moved beyond that point seems to be indicated by the heated nature of the rhetoric directed toward me, by Dr. King's references to "my" (his) board, by the vast increase in the intensity of administrative attempts to place negative material in my file, by my recently lowered performance rating, by the attempts to undermine my courses, by my new "schedule from hell," and by the stacking of board meetings with individuals primed to speak against me. These strategies—all used successfully in the past—suggest that the administration intends to ask the trustees to sit in judgment on me. And at least some trustees seem to be caught up in emotions which make them anxious to do so.

I'm enclosing drafts of two grievances, and a document I will be attaching to my 1990-1991 annual evaluation. Whether or not I file the grievances in their present form, the material should help clarify the issues if (when?) you are called upon to support administrative action against me. I'm willing to lay out my position ahead of time because I have confidence in your fairmindedness once you know all the facts.

In the meantime, could we concentrate on the issue at hand? I understand Dr. King is to write me a letter in response to my letter to you. I assume that, for strategic purposes, it will arrive a day or two before the board meeting, leaving me little or no time to respond.

I stand by what I wrote, including the Page Three comments related to violations of the Fair Labor Standards Act which one of the trustees asked about.

My I respectfully request that you withhold judgment until the evidence is in?

(Exhibit #152)

Notwithstanding the fact that a month earlier the trustees had officially abolished McCrory's position, he continued to stuff my file, writing me up for not being where he thought I ought to be, and for not showing him the respect he thought he was due. He also continued to visit my classes. After the fifth or sixth such visit, two friends on the faculty, Alison Pittman and Beverly

Slaughter—both female, both black—told me that McCrory
had never been inside their classrooms.

On the 21st of April, 1992, McCrory wrote a memo to
Aitken:

> As you know, I did not recommend Marion for
> renewal of contract. With his most recent behav-
> ior and Reprimand I strongly recommend the
> issue be put back on the table for discussion. If we
> get sued, we get sued. However I strongly believe
> are [sic] case is solid. I'm running thin on patience
> with this guy.

(Exhibit #77)

STUD STEVE, BIG DADDY BOB

Events got more soap opera-like daily. Provost Aitken
would come by my office and make small talk (for the
benefit of any electronic bugs) while writing out what he
really wanted to say on paper. When I'd drop by his
office, he'd turn on the television, then talk softly below
its volume level. Sometimes, we'd talk in hallways.

Bob never tired of reminding me of the depth of his
friendship with me. I'd tell him I appreciated and enjoyed
him, but that we both knew that, if push came to shove
and he had to choose between friendship for me and loyalty to King, he'd deliver my head on a platter. He'd
deny it, and sometimes I'd almost believe him. After all,
we'd shared scores of breakfasts, I'd heard hundreds of
times about his true feelings for King, he told me frequently of his frustration at not being the right gender—
with the accompanying physiological equipment—to facilitate his rapid promotion at the College. Our relationship
was far more than professional. He frequently called my

home at night to talk. He and his wife and Joy and I had gone out to dinner together. All this made his declarations of undying friendship almost believable. But I couldn't set aside the dozens of stories of "friends" he had left swinging in the wind when his own skin was involved.

Aitken called me into his office first thing one morning, purportedly for small talk. The phone rang. Motioning for me to keep quiet, he answered it and mouthed "Bert Purga" to let me know who was on the other end. It soon became apparent (Bob wasn't much of an actor) that the call was prearranged. With exaggerated care, he repeated what he was hearing as if trying to clarify it in his own mind. From Aitken: "Oh, really? Is that right? Brady's on thin ice?"

At 10:15 on the 11th of May I was once again in Aitken's office, the television was on and the volume was up as we sat at a small conference table. He made miscellaneous small talk in a normal conversational tone, but mostly he wrote.

First message: McCrory was out to get both of us. Second message: Legal action was being planned for me. Third message: He'd call me at home that night. Fourth message: McCrory had to go, and he had some stuff for me that ought to do the job.

He handed me a plain envelope, told me not to lay it down, and said it should cut McCrory's throat.

I went back to my office, opened the envelope, and thought perhaps he was right. What he'd given me were copies of interoffice E-mail messages from McCrory to a female employee in the administration building. The messages weren't recent, but they were, at the least, pretty damning for an "educator" on the public payroll to have written on company time. I wondered how many minutes it would have taken the administration to throw me out the door if I had sent similar interoffice messages.

On the 26th of September, 1990, at 1:42 p.m., the
man who wanted to fire me for misconduct wrote to a
woman in the registrar's office:

From: STEVAN McCRORY

SIX TO EIGHT INCHES, WET AND SOME-
TIMES STICKY—TAKES YOUR MIND OFF OF
HEADACHES—MAY NOT GET RID OF THE
ACHE BUT THE HEAD SHOULD BE GOOD.

(Exhibit #159)

Eight minutes later:

MIGHT BE BETTER WITH A JACKET. YOU
DRAW ATTENTION TO YOURSELF THAT
YOU MIGHT NOT WANT TO DRAW. IF YOU
DON'T MIND SOMEBODY GIVING YOU A LIP
LOCK ON YOUR BREAST THEN GO FOR IT.
PERHAPS YOU DON'T MIND IF OTHERS SEE
WHAT YOU HAVE TO OFFER.

(Ibid.)

On October the 1st:

THANKS A LOT. TAYLOR [Probably Bill Taylor,
head of Student Services] ASKED ME OUTSIDE
IF I WAS INPUTTING MINIMESTER STUFF
WITH YOU AND I TOLD HIM ALL YOU DID
WAS EXPLAINED [sic] WHAT SCREEN FOR
ME TO USE AND I WAS ON MY WAY TO THE

OFFICE TO DO IT MYSELF. THANKS AND I
OWE YOU. TS IS STILL HERE BUT I HAVE TO
GO NOW. WILL SEE YOU TOMORROW. I
ALWAYS DAY DREAM ABOUT YOU. ESPE-
CIALLY WHEN TAYLOR IS TALKING.

(Ibid.)

The last of the memos was dated October 2nd:

A HEARTY GOOD MORNING TO MY FAVOR-
ITE BCC PERSON. MET WITH YOU AT ABOUT
420AM. SORRY I TORE THE SLIP—COULDN'T
WAIT—WAS TRYING TO BE POLITE BUT GOT
OVER EXCITED.

(Ibid.)

Just before the May meeting of the trustees, I was
walking across campus when Director of Employee Relations Bob Craig hailed me. "I was just on my way out to
your house to drop this off," he said, handing me a package.

In an envelope was a copy of the presentations prepared weeks earlier by McCrory, Lawton and Craig for
oral presentation at the April board meeting (the ones
mailed the day after Matheny's warning to the trustees
that listening to those same remarks could disqualify
them from a role in any hearing involving me).

The package contained 19 pages of comment and rebuttal of my yes-I've-been-harassed letter to the trustees.
It was so loaded with detail it would have taken me a
week to respond adequately. And just as I had predicted
in my earlier letter to the trustees, I'd been handed the

package too late to prepare before the next meeting of
the trustees. With no time to gather documentation, it
was either merely my word against Craig's, Lawton's and
McCrory's, or I'd have to focus on just a couple of the
issues for which backup material was immediately accessible.

On the 12th of May, I wrote the trustees:

> As you'll recall, during your March meeting,
> a request was made for information about admin-
> istrative harassment of employees.
>
> I responded, and for my time and trouble a
> good portion of your April meeting was devoted to
> attacking, not my response, but my character and
> credibility. At that meeting, after talk of "slan-
> der," "legal action," and "dismissal," the trus-
> tees instructed Dr. King to respond to my letter.
>
> He passed responsibility on to Director of Em-
> ployee Relations Robert Craig, whose sarcastically
> titled "Response to Latest List of Mr. Brady's
> Claims" was handed to me Monday afternoon,
> May 11. As I predicted, I am left with almost no
> time to respond.
>
> Perhaps, however, that's for the best. The
> sheer weight of Mr. Craig's material is impres-
> sive, and will probably go far toward creating a
> convincing impression of thoroughness. If I had
> more time, I'd be tempted to answer and docu-
> ment in such detail few might have plowed
> through what I would have had to say.
>
> For the third time: I'll not back off on any
> claim I've made. But since I've only two hours
> before I'm due at Brevard Chorale rehearsal, let
> me deal, for illustrative purposes, with one "little
> claim" and one "big claim." We can go on from

there later if—or more probably when—the legal need arises.

Little Claim

I was the only teacher on the Melbourne campus whose classroom was visited by Tace Crouse. My rather cryptic-sounding comment at the time of that visit apparently caused Ms. Crouse to realize that she had perhaps made a tactical, potentially embarrassing mistake in singling me out.

So what did she do at the last minute to cover herself? Note carefully her choice of words. She doesn't say she actually visited anyone else's classroom. I don't know what she did for Randy Eastep, but she "observed" Pat Jones and Rosa Poehler from the hallway later on that Friday, then sent them notes to "document" her "observations." She never set foot inside their classrooms . . .

"Big" Claim (Violations of Fair Labor Standards Act)

I've quite a file for this one. However, careful selection of a very few documents (not newspaper accounts which were manipulated from the outset) should clarify the picture.

I said:

(a) Hourly employees worked overtime without overtime pay,

(b) Pressure was put on them to settle for comp time,

(c) Campuses were left without security for many hours.

(Exhibit #153)

I then provided complete documentation: copies of employee time sheets, a copy of the form given to employees that provided space for them to write in hours of comp time but no space for money owed them, schedule sheets for two campuses showing the dates, shifts and times when no security personnel were on campus, and a copy of a log on the entire National Labor Relations Board matter kept by Christine Suleski. (I noted in passing that "Ms. Suleski, a 14-year employee of the College, a single parent with a dependent, almost certainly the most competent and dedicated of all BCC staff employees, was casually fired by you." [The trustees].)

I told the trustees they didn't have to take my word for any of this. On the matter of Tace Crouse's visits, I said, "Please call Rosa Poehler and/or Pat Jones. Ms. Poehler will tell you that she has never met Ms. Crouse. Ms. Jones—if pushed—may tell you how she and other faculty reacted to the note she received from Ms. Crouse subsequent to her "observation" from a hallway. For verification of my version of the Fair Labor Standards Act matter, I told the trustees to contact Richard Parham, a 21-year BCC retired security officer. I gave them his phone number, and said that he had other details they might find "interesting."

None of those whose names and phone numbers I provided were ever contacted by trustees or trustee representatives to discuss whether it was I or the administration that was lying.

I continued:

Much of the rest of Mr. Craig's letter is made
up of material generated by Mr. McCrory. I won't
dignify it with a response. Document package #4
[McCrory's E-mail messages] is a small, early
example of Mr. McCrory's voluminous work. It
may provide some insight into his professionalism,
character, and interests. It may also shed considerable light on how he spends his time on campus when he is not concentrating on his primary
assignment, which for several months now has
been to end my career and send me the way [the
trustees] just sent Tom Ward, Craig Edwards,
Christine Suleski, Shawn Smith, and others.

(Ibid.)

I concluded, parenthetically:

(I don't enjoy this level of thing at all, and I
will block out the names of females involved on
all copies of interoffice memoranda excepting
those which go to trustees. But the board's unwillingness to engage in genuine dialogue with its
own employees, its years of support for an administration entirely preoccupied with power and self-
aggrandizement, its collective refusal to see the
viciousness and moral bankruptcy of this administration, necessitates the rather brutal dumping of
at least a little of the masses of material which
have come into my hands, material which would
surely have gone to the trustees had they been
seen as genuinely committed to the welfare of the
institution. Whenever I'm tempted to soften my
stand, I remember the human devastation this
administration has left and continues to leave in
its wake.)

For verification of Mr. McCrory's version of
what constitutes truth, with myriad, specific incidents cited, I'll be happy to provide the names and
telephone numbers of forty or fifty faculty members.

If you'd now care to move on to other matters
discussed (or conveniently ignored) in Mr. Craig's
"Response to the Latest List of Mr. Brady's
Claims," I'll be happy to oblige.

(Ibid.)

"HE'S FIRED. WE'RE JUST WAITING FOR DUE PROCESS."

In April, Alan Thornquest, Tom Ward and I had
called the leadership of the United Faculty of Florida in
Tallahassee asking for help. On the 27th, the UFF sent
Tallahassee attorney Tom Brooks down to hear what we
had to say. We met at Fat Boy's Restaurant in Cocoa. He
took voluminous notes, told us to inventory our personnel
files, and initial and date the pages. He said he'd tell our
story to the decision makers at the UFF.

In the middle of the afternoon on Thursday, May 14,
1992, I was sitting in the BCC Melbourne library reading
professional journals. Provost Aitken and Director of
Employee Relations Bob Craig came to my table and
handed me a document. (I've since wondered if they
would have been doing what they were doing if they
could have known that both would soon suffer near-fatal
heart attacks.)

I glanced at the document, went to a pay phone and
called Tom Brooks in Tallahassee.

The official minutes of the board of trustees put it
this way:

Dr. King distributed a resolution to the Board members. Mr. Matheny stated this is a petition filed by the President of the College under Chapter 6A-140411(6) of the Board of Education Regulations to not renew a contract of a tenured professor. This petition requires a due process hearing wherein the College Board would sit as a fair and impartial quasi-judicial body to determine whether or not the charges referenced in this petition should be sustained. The affected instructor has twenty days to respond to the petition. Mr. Matheny stated the Board would not officially accept the petition until June 11, the regularly scheduled Board meeting. He stated the Board should not discuss the petition with any person who is part of the College community. Mr. Matheny stated he would serve as counsel and advisor for the Board. Mr. Matheny reported no action is required by the Board at this time.

(Exhibit #51)

Florida Today said:

"BCC Files Petition to Fire Instructor"

Brevard Community College President Maxwell King has filed a petition to fire Marion Brady, a long-time critic of King's administration.

Under state regulations, the college's board of trustees must consider accepting the petition at its next meeting and set a date, said Joe Matheny, the board's lawyer. Matheny also advised the board not to publicly discuss the petition until that time.

Brady was presented with the petition at his office Thursday, just prior to the board's 4 p.m. meeting, said Bob Craig, employee relations director. However, Brady did not attend the meeting.

Brady said late Tuesday, "I hope the justice system works as it's supposed to work. (If it does) I have nothing to worry about."

According to the petition, King accuses Brady of misconduct, insubordination and willful neglect of his duties. The accusations include:

■ "Failing and refusing to be present in his office during posted student advisement hours on a number of occasions."

■ "Using class time to voice complaints against the board of trustees and/or administrative personnel of the college, rather than to provide instructional services to students."

■ "Failing and refusing to attend employee-related meetings with his dean."

Earlier this month, Brady filed grievances with his supervisors. He accuses administrators of harassment and unfair treatment. He claims his supervisor has evaluated his teaching performance more frequently than other faculty members and his class schedule has been changed for "no professionally valid reason."

(Florida Today, *5-15-92*)

Associate Vice President for Human Resources and then-mayor of Cocoa Beach Robert Lawton said it best of all: "He's fired. We're just waiting for due process."

FRIENDS

Support for me came from everywhere. Faculty members and students called and asked what they could do to help. The American Civil Liberties Union wrote a letter protesting the College administration's action, arguing that transcripts of board meetings, correspondence and other materials "indicate the trustees have prejudices that make it inappropriate for the board to assume the role of jury." John Manning, a personal friend, contacted attorney William Horner, who worked for NASA, and asked him to advise me. And on the 1st of July, the United Faculty of Florida sued on behalf of Alan Thornquest, Tom Ward and me.

In an article titled "**3 sue, saying BCC violated rights,**" *Florida Today* reporter Jim Ash wrote:

A Brevard Community College instructor and two former faculty members filed a lawsuit Wednesday charging college officials with violating their civil rights.

The suit, filed in Brevard circuit court, alleges the men lost their jobs or are facing dismissal because they were union organizers or critics of college administrators.

The suit names BCC President Maxwell King, several other administrators and the board of trustees as defendants.

Termination procedures taken against the three men violated their rights to free speech, the suit charges.

The suit seeks to halt termination procedures being taken against sociology teacher Marion Brady and asks that the court reinstate and award back wages to former counselor Alan Thornquest and former sociology teacher Thomas

Ward. The suit also asks unspecified damages and reimbursement for court costs.

Bob Craig, BCC's director of employee relations, said he had not seen the lawsuit and declined to comment on the specific reasons the men were terminated.

However, Craig denied the college acted against the men because of their criticisms of the administration or their union activities. "Each of the three cases (is) individual. There is no correlation to union activity and free speech, both of which the college respects," he said.

Brady, who was hired in 1976, has been charged by administrators with insubordination. He faces a dismissal hearing July 28 before King and the trustees.

The men lost or are losing their jobs because "they have been longtime enemies of Maxwell King," said their attorney, Tom Brooks of Tallahassee.

Mr. Brady has thrown caution to the wind and stood on his principles, and sometimes there's a price to pay for that," Brooks said.

Brady, a member of a union bargaining team since 1983, has railed against King in guest columns in *Florida Today* and union newsletters.

The suit says he "assisted" college security guards in winning compensation for unpaid overtime. A U.S. Department of Labor investigation led to the compensation. Federal investigators declined to name a confidential informant who prompted the investigation.

Ward, a former member of the accreditation committee of the Southern Association of Colleges [and Schools], conducted a survey of faculty members in 1990 and compiled the reports critical of King.

From 1980 to 1988, Thornquest was the membership chairman of the Brevard Community College Federation of Teachers Local 1847 and in 1982 helped organize the faculty in the Division of Allied Health, the suit states.

When Thornquest was denied tenure in 1983, he sued King, charging him with violating his constitutional rights. That December, Thornquest was granted a continuing contract . . .

(Florida Today, 7-2-92)

The UFF engaged a second attorney, John Chamblee of Tampa, to work with Tom Brooks on our case. BCC trustees had hoped to conduct my hearing on July 28, but Chamblee and Brooks filed a motion accepted at a July 9 meeting of the trustees that delayed the action until September—exactly 40 years from the time I walked into my first class in a rural Ohio classroom as a full-time teacher.

Chamblee spoke briefly at the July 9 meeting, responding to a query from Simpkins about the probable length of the hearing. Simpkins wanted some assurance that ending my 40-year career would take only a day or a day and a half.

Chamblee said he'd make no such commitment. "You and your people have piled the sink full of dirty pots and pans," he said, "and we're going to stay here until I've scrubbed every one of them clean." Soon thereafter, Brooks and Chamblee began deposing witnesses.

By this time, Bill Horner had requested a stack of documents from King, the BCC administration, and the trustees. He told them the law was clear, that anyone sitting as judge or jury had to come to the case unbiased, and, on the basis of audio tapes of BCC board of trustee

meetings to which he had listened, none of the trustees
met the criteria.

A September 10, 1992 letter from Horner to the BCC
administration was typical:

RE: PRA [Public Records Act] Brady Termination
Hearing—Possible Disqualification of Board Members

Some *3 weeks ago*, I wrote you regarding the
alleged attendance of Bernie Simpkins at the
5/30/90 board meeting.

Under PRA, I requested documentation regarding the appointment, etc., of the now-chairman of
the BOT.

I have heard nothing from the board, its secretary, its attorney, the president of the College, or
anyone.

As I stated on 8/20/92, the requested documentation may have a direct bearing on the question
of disqualification/recusal involved in the Brady
hearing scheduled for 9/17/92.

Please advise ASAP, as time is running out re
justice being done in this matter.

There was no response. During my hearing, I testified
that board chairman Simpkins had been present. There
was no denial.

Attorney Horner also began a long and fruitless
attempt to get information under the Public Records Act
about some of the matters I had tried, without success, to
bring to public attention.

In the next few months, before becoming seriously ill,
Horner filed between dozens and dozens of requests for
information under Florida's Public Records Act. Such
requests are supposed to be honored in a reasonable

length of time—"reasonable" ordinarily meaning two or three days. Only a handful brought a response; almost none resulted in complete disclosure of the requested documents.

STRAIGHT STORY

The first deposition taken in preparation for my hearing was from ex-dean Dr. Ann Thomas, on August 4, 1992. After two years of frozen salary, and after being returned to teacher status without the tenure she had acquired before becoming an administrator, Thomas knew her days at BCC were numbered. She began to apply for positions elsewhere and, shortly before giving her deposition, had accepted an administrative post at a community college in Longview, Washington.

We talked at length the day before her deposition. She was convinced that, even though she had resigned, King was so vindictive he would continue to do everything he could to make life difficult for her. She had already detected what she thought was a pattern. What she felt was happening was that when she applied for a position that represented a lateral move, VP Purga, who was listed as a reference, was called and gave her a favorable recommendation. When she applied for a job that represented a promotion—say, a vice president slot—King was called. He would not recommend her. Sometime later, she verified her suspicion.

Thomas had a new, lateral job, but she was apprehensive about what King might be able to do to cause her difficulties in that position as well as in any future position. Nevertheless, there were certain matters she hoped would emerge in the course of her deposition. With her permission, I took notes during our conversation. Here's a summary:

■ I had been disciplined for failing to adhere
strictly to student advisement hours. Although
Dr. Thomas said that most faculty didn't consistently observe their student advisement schedule,
the issue had never previously been raised.

■ I had thought King always used a go-
between in matters that could come back to haunt
him legally. However, she told me that this
wasn't always the case. Once, she said, she had an
hour-and-a-half session with King devoted exclu-
sively to his asking her what she intended to do to
shut me up. Among much else, he kept asking her
if I was a good teacher, and she kept saying yes.
King told her that every time she said "yes," her
credibility with him went down.

■ VP Bert Purga told her to give me a tough-
er schedule (a schedule with more preparations).
Feeling that she had no alternative, this she did,
despite the fact that my previous schedule had for
years resulted in class sizes far above the institutional average.

Was there, I asked her, indisputable pressure on her
to attempt to block my freedom to speak and write publicly about problems at the College? Her response was an
unequivocal yes.

I'm not certain whether it was in this conversation or
another that Thomas and I talked about why certain of
her sex seemed to fare so well in BCC administrative
circles. She told me she thought it was a simple trade-off.
Both parties got what they wanted. These matters are, of
course, much gossiped about in faculty circles, fed by
stories such as the one alleging that such-and-such a
female in administrative ascendancy entertained a top-
level administrator in her room until just before dawn.
Many faculty believe that, eventually, a "George and

Lurleen Wallace arrangement" will provide the College's governance.

MORE STORIES

Perhaps the best source of straight information about the issues surrounding King's firing of Alan, Tom and me were the sworn affidavits submitted by ex-administrators.

One came from ex-dean Joanne Nicholson. Nicholson had been hired as a BCC counselor in 1969, was promoted to Dean of Students at the Melbourne campus in 1976, and became Dean of Students on the Cocoa campus in 1979.

I didn't work for Dean Nicholson, but her affidavit speaks to issues that bore indirectly on my case. She had, for example, in 1983, recommended that Alan be placed on continuing contract. Apparently in retaliation for Alan's having recruited 10 new members for the faculty union, King demanded that Nicholson's recommendation of Alan for continuing contract be withdrawn. She said it like this:

3. In 1983, I recommended Mr. Thornquest for continuing contract for the 1983-84 academic year. However, pursuant to Dr. King's recommendation, he was actually placed on another annual contract.

4. I completed an evaluation of Mr. Thornquest's performance for the 1983-84 period and rated his performance as excellent. After I completed his evaluation, I was called into the office of my Provost, Dr. Kay Heimer, and was advised that I was to lower his evaluation in the area of attitude. I advised her that Mr. Thornquest was

an excellent counselor, that in my professional
opinion this evaluation accurately reflected his
performance, and that "attitude" was not one of
the criteria to be rated. I suggested that if she disagreed with my assessment, there were procedures by which her disagreement could be reflected. She further stated that Mr. Thornquest had a
lawsuit pending against the College and reiter-
ated that I needed to lower his evaluation. I refused to do so.

5. Dr. Heimer stated that I left her no alternative but to reflect my refusal to change
Mr. Thornquest's evaluation in my [own] evaluation. As a result, I was rated as below expectations in the area of ability to evaluate employees.

(Affidavit notarized 7-29-93)

King frowned on administrators fraternizing with
other administrators away from the College. He was even
less happy about administrators fraternizing with faculty.
And, if the faculty member with which the administrator
was friendly wasn't liked by King, action was called for:

8. I am and was during my employment at
the College a personal friend of June England, a
faculty member and vocal union member. Following my involuntary transfer to Dean of College
Wide Student Services at the Cocoa campus, I was
cautioned by Steve Megregian and Joe Keller;
they stated that I had been seen having lunch
with June England and cautioned me about continuing to do so. I advised them that I had no

intention of discontinuing my association with
Ms. England.

(Ibid.)

Over the years, King and other administrators
advanced many "reasons" for my criticism of the situation at the College, including mental instability, jealousy
of King, frustration at not achieving to my father's level
(my father was for several years president of Shenandoah
College in Virginia), and resentment at having to comply
with various College policies. Reading Nicholson's affidavit, I learned of yet another "reason" for what was
considered my unacceptable attitude:

> 10. As an administrator, I attended the admin-
> istrative staff meetings which were conducted by
> Dr. King. During these meetings, comments were
> made about Marion Brady. One comment that I
> recall is that Dr. King stated that Marion Brady
> was disgruntled because he had published a text-
> book that the College wouldn't use.

(Ibid.)

This was news to me. I've written two textbooks, both
published by Prentice-Hall. Both were for secondary level
and were inappropriate for use by college students.
Perhaps King was referring to a more recent work,
What's Worth Teaching? If such was the case, he was
again far off base. This was a professional book, intended
for a relatively few individuals working in the field of
curriculum theory and design. As far as I know, no
course related to curriculum theory is taught at the com-

munity college level anywhere in America, and even if
that weren't the case, the book was not in appropriate
form for use by college students.

Nicholson concluded her affidavit with an explanation
of events preceding what she characterized as her "forced
retirement" in 1991. She said that students on the Palm
Bay campus, reacting to news stories about BCC budget
cuts, organized a protest rally. Following College policy,
they completed a form explaining what they were protesting and the campus location where they intended to
demonstrate. The form called for the signature of a dean.
Nicholson, seeing no reason to block students from exer-
cising their constitutional rights, signed the form.

Almost   immediately,   she   was   confronted   by
Dr. Marion Campbell, Provost of the Palm Bay campus,
and told that she was "in serious trouble," that she was
considered "a troublemaker" by the administration, and
that Dr. King wanted her to resign.

Nicholson protested that she had been approving such
rallies and student activities for years. Her explanations
weren't considered acceptable by the administration.

Her forced resignation came just two years before she
would have been eligible for full retirement benefits.

The last item on her affidavit (#15), affirmed a view
shared by those most familiar with the College and
argued during my hearing. She said, "It was (her) experience during 22 years at Brevard Community College that
Dr. King's method of dealing with employees who fell
into his disfavor was by eliminating their positions."

More calls concern problems at LCCC

Call in Columbia 752-5295

Lake City Reporter

CALLER: I don't know about you, Columbia County, but I think that the time has come that there should be a complete investigation of LCCC. We need to replace some of the people out there that can not mak decision, rightly, as to employee keep digging, board members, you'll find out more.

* * *

CALLER: Dr. Heimer has pro over and over again that she has her personal interest at heart

Lake City Community College. I say it's time for Lake City Communi College to be thinking toward a n president. One that has education and for the community a

PBCC gran still mired in confusic

Final audit report doesn't clear DBCC

By DONNA CALLEA
Daytona Beach News-Journal

nselves, but nly on college o Dr. [Ed] Eissey delib them.

"We don't call him Pin ing," says Rep. [Carol] Ha

at ther rence o statem

State audit criticizes HCC bookkeeping

BY STEVE KANIGHER

ments and computerized ledger since July 1, 19 though college officials sa response to a preliminary hey had done so and no

BCC dema

Facul

Adminis confide

The bu is desig clearly

Part-tin no thre

Union a bring r

Admini effecti

Source: B

eavy community colleges?

Tampa Tribune

wton Chiles' pledge to end waste
ling in government has taken him
ty-college system.

colleges traditionally escape scruti-
iends in high places. Chief among
Speaker T.K. Wetherell, a former
ge administrator. And — could it
— just before or after running for
islators landed jobs at community

irprise that Doug Cook, Chiles'
er, draws from community colleg-
naking. He offers this illustration
camline state bureaucracies:
unity college, only 10 professors
$53,000. None earns more than
administrative offices, however,
ministrators earning more than
ries of 10 top $80,000.

• • •

parison, the Health and Rehabili-
rict based in Tampa is a 4,000-

employee outfit. *None* of its administrators earns as
much as HCC's executive vice president for academic affairs — including the physician who is
deputy district administrator for health. Furthermore, the two HRS "subdistrict administrators" —
one responsible for Hillsborough and Manatee, the
other for Highlands, Hardee, and Polk — make less
than $50,000.

Nor is it uncommon to find an administrator at
a community college making more than his or her
counterpart at a state university.

• • •

(Incidentally, at HCC, the Tribune's request for
information bounced from administrator to administrator: the community relations director, the
institutional advancement director, the president,
the executive vice president for academic affairs, the
budget director, and the comptroller.)

Perhaps community colleges can come up with
a cogent explanation of why so many administrators are so well paid. It's time someone asked.

survey results
ntion of board

	Agree	Disagree
s	12%	88%
	4%	96%
	20%	80%
	86%	14%
	14%	86%

ty:

v

FLORIDA TODAY

BCC president 'dismisses' complaints

By Roni Bea Kayne
FLORIDA TODAY

Brevard Community College
President Maxwell King says
there are no problems at the
school. Faculty and student
leaders say problems are being
ignored.

Part VI

AN EQUAL OPPORTUNITY EMPLOYER?

Universally respected, and with nearly a half-century of combined service to the College, Ann Thomas and Joanne Nicholson could not have been more credible witnesses. A third ex-administrator, Jasper Trigg, although not a long-time employee, was no less credible.

When McCrory went to BCC's Melbourne campus as dean of the liberal arts division, Jasper Trigg was already there as dean of the mathematics and science division. Both came to the College from outside academia, both were deans on the same campus, and both were African-American. But there the parallels ended. Those who thought highly of King for his supposed contribution to equal racial opportunity should have looked closely at Jasper Trigg's career at BCC.

McCrory came from the enlisted ranks of the military. Trigg came to BCC from the personnel department of the U.S. Internal Revenue Service. McCrory was relatively young. Trigg was nearing 60. McCrory's behavior was, in the eyes of those who worked for him, tasteless and crude. Trigg was, without exception, considered a perfect gentleman. McCrory's administrative skills were not apparent to the members of his department. Trigg was generally considered to be the most competent administrator ever to hold the math-science position. McCrory got off on the right foot; he was willing to be used by the King administration. Trigg got off on the wrong foot; he was not willing to do what he considered ethically indefensible.

Trigg's integrity and competence were never questioned; stories about McCrory's abuse of his position were never ending. When, in preparation for my hearing, I began collecting information about the man who was constantly accusing me of unprofessionalism—McCrory—I got a stack of written notes from fellow faculty members. Here's one of them:

The deal with the student assistant, my student assistant? Recently I was sort of surprised about that because she is a nice little kid. I mean I like the girl and what really frosts me is that she just went down and sold those books and kept the money and the books were bought for her by McCrory. What a deal! The point is that she works for a doctor, has one job and works for us as a student assistant. But she came in one day and she got real friendly with McCrory through Carol Marx [sometime secretary to McCrory]. Carol Marx used to work down there, you know, and she and Carol were good friends. She was spending a lot of time with McCrory and I was kind of worried about that. But I never said anything. I thought, well, you know, it's Carol.

But anyway she came back one day and she said, "You won't believe this." And I said, "What? I'll believe anything." She said, "Look at this," and she showed it to me and it was a memo. She was down there complaining to McCrory, just sitting there eating popcorn and watching television with him, I guess. [McCrory had television and a popcorn machine in his office.] And she said she didn't have any money to buy her books and he said, "No problem." He wrote a note to the bookstore saying, "Please allow [the student assistant] to charge her books to this division account, plus refund any money she's already spent on books."

I looked at the memo, and she went and got her books on the division account.

I told Bob Aitken and he took care of it. I was in his office and he called the bookstore and said, "I want a list of every student who's been allowed to purchase books through division accounts." He said, "What really worries me is that this may be the tip of the iceberg." I said, "I never even thought about that."

I don't know if there were others, but that's what he said to me. And in this time of great need.

Later on, when the term was over, she sold her books and pocketed the money. Although I like Tina, I didn't think that was appropriate.

According to another faculty member, George Cornelius, McCrory offered a woman whom he liked—a woman without even a bachelor's degree and with only a fourth grade English education—a foreign language adjunct faculty position. When Cornelius insisted that the woman simply wasn't qualified for the job, McCrory three times gave him a direct order to hire her. He also ordered Cornelius not to discuss the matter with the other full-time language faculty member, Tom Morrison, or the campus provost, Robert Aitken.

The whole ordeal so disturbed Cornelius that he engaged an attorney.

The matter wasn't finally resolved until Cornelius took a delegation of faculty to the administration, laid out the facts, and let it be known that he had hired a lawyer.

According to faculty member Jeff Neill, Joy Diamond, a student of his acquaintance, ran into McCrory in the hallway outside McCrory's office. Seeing that she wasn't feeling well, McCrory told her that he had a couch in his

office, and that if she'd come in and lie down they could
find out what her "real problem" was.

Cindy Batten, a student assistant, said that when she
told McCrory she needed additional hours so as to make
more money, he told her that he could arrange more
work for her if she'd be "more friendly." She said his
meaning was clear.

Despite the glaring differences in their performance
and professionalism, in the summer of 1992 McCrory was
promoted to dean of the Patrick AFB branch, and Trigg
was fired.

Within weeks of McCrory's being sent to the Patrick
Center, I got a call from his secretary, Melinda Ayala,
asking for advice about whom she might contact for information about harassment suits and legal action. She
cited as an example of the problem an instance in which
McCrory told her to approach another female of Hispanic
descent.

"You know that Puerto Rican talk," he had said.
"Go ask her if she's married." He wanted Melinda to try
to arrange a date with the woman for him. After repeated failed attempts to get the BCC administration to do
something about the problem, the situation became so intolerable that Ms. Ayala's husband and her doctor insisted that she quit. This she did, and instituted legal
action against McCrory and the College. When I last
heard, the matter was in litigation.

Jasper Trigg, after a difficult job search, was hired in
an administrative position by Brevard County, with offices in Viera, and soon became head of several departments.

Here are excerpts from an affidavit Jasper Trigg
voluntarily submitted to one of my attorneys, John
Chamblee:

2. Upon my assignment as Academic Dean for Math/Science, I met with President Maxwell King and Robert Lawton at which time I was advised that there was a problem with the division secretary, Christine Suleski. There was concern expressed that Ms. Suleski was controlling the Division and making decisions that were not within the realms of her designated responsibilities.

3. I was advised during this meeting with Dr. King and Mr. Lawton that I had two options in dealing with Ms. Suleski. I could transfer her or move to dismiss her. I chose neither and opted to work with her.

4. I found Ms. Suleski to be a very dedicated, loyal, enthusiastic, professional and competent employee. Due to continued absences of the previous dean, Ms. Suleski had made decisions to ensure that the Division ran smoothly and had apparently done so effectively.

5. It was later revealed to me by Dr. Bert Purga that Ms. Suleski had been linked with Marion Brady's activities and it was perceived that she had assisted him with typing and other activities related to his publications. It was further perceived that Ms. Suleski and Mr. Brady were friends.

6. Following my decision to retain Ms. Suleski, I was approached by Mr. Lawton, Dr. Purga and Dr. Aitken regarding what they perceived as continued disrespect for Dr. King by Ms. Suleski. Dr. Purga stated that I should consider getting rid of Ms. Suleski. I advised that she was doing a fine job and I had no such intentions. It is my belief that my handling of Ms. Suleski and my refusal to terminate her employment had a direct impact on the termination of my employment from Brevard Community College.

7. On March 5, 1992, I was called into
Dr. Aitken's office, with Dean Whitehead present
as witness, and advised that effective "immediately" my duties as Dean were relinquished and that
I would report to his office to be assigned special
projects until June, 1992, when my contract
ended. I was advised that after June, I would no
longer have a position at the College. The stated
reason for the change in responsibilities was that
the College was being reorganized and the positions of Academic Dean were being eliminated to
improve communications. I was informed that I
had no supervisory responsibility over my department and it was clear to me that the change was
effective immediately.

8. I was also present at the faculty meeting
on March 5, 1992, where Dr. Aitken announced
that effective immediately, the Deans would no
longer be in charge of their respective divisions
and would be assigned to his office for special projects.

(Affidavit notarized 6-16-93)

Trigg then said that he was given nothing to do; that
a check with Ann Thomas, dean of liberal arts on the
Cocoa campus, indicated she was being similarly treated;
and that discussions with Purga and King resulted in his
being told that "there didn't appear that there was any
position open" for him.

His sworn affidavit continued:

12. When I heard that Mr. McCrory was going
to be retained by the College I approached
Dr. Purga   who   advised   that   based   on

Mr. McCrory's background there would be a position for him. At that time I had thirty years of managerial experience with the Federal government and academic institutions, yet no position was available for me.

13. I was later offered a position in an outreach program on an hourly basis with no benefits. Dr. King commented that perhaps after I demonstrated my abilities, "someone may pick me up." I subsequently obtained my current job with Brevard County in August, 1992.

14. After McCrory's arrival at the Melbourne campus I had several conversations with him respecting several issues. Mr. McCrory advised me that he was "going to kick some butt"; although no name was mentioned, it was evident to me from the context of our discussions that he was referring to Marion Brady. Mr. McCrory was known to me to be a "head hunter" whose task was to find a way to obtain the removal of Mr. Brady from employment.

15. In late March or early April, 1992, faculty members advised me that Mr. McCrory appeared to be involved in evaluations, specifically of Marion Brady. I approached Mr. McCrory and inquired what role he was playing and he stated that he was going to do what he had to do and that in regards to Mr. Brady, he reported directly to Dr. King. He further stated that he had an open door to Dr. King.

16. Mr. McCrory also discussed with me his sending of "E" mail messages that contained sexual overtures. Mr. McCrory stated to me that he had sent the "E Mails" and that in doing so he had used poor judgment. [McCrory testified under oath that he hadn't sent the messages.]

17. Mr. McCrory was not well respected
among faculty and other personnel. I have been
advised by faculty and have personal knowledge
that Mr. McCrory treated people with disrespect
and used profanity regardless of who was present.
I also received periodic complaints about his methods of dealing with personnel. Mr. McCrory was
perceived by members of the BCC faculty with
whom he had confrontations to be untruthful and
untrustworthy.

(Ibid.)

McCrory was alleged to be an opportunistic exploiter
of the race issue. A woman who worked with him for several years at Patrick Air Force Base told me that if he
got in trouble, he'd try to use the race issue to his
advantage. Appreciating this fact, Trigg concluded:

18. I came to know Marion Brady while at the
Melbourne campus and through all my contacts
with Mr. Brady, I never perceived him to be
racially biased.

(Ibid.)

HOUSE ARREST

If I had been teaching in Brevard's public schools and
faced an administrative charge, Florida's laws would
have afforded me some protection.

First, I could have asked to meet with the superintendent for an informal review of the charge of unsatisfac-
tory performance.

Second, I could have asked for transfer to a different supervisor in another location during the following year.

Third, during that year, the administration would have been required by law to provide me with assistance and inservice education to deal with my "problem." They would also have been obligated to evaluate me periodically and give me written evaluations informing me of my progress or lack of it.

Fourth, at least six weeks before the end of the employment year, I'd have been told if I weren't going to be offered a new contract.

Fifth, if such was the case, I could then demand a hearing before the full school board. If I thought I wouldn't get a fair and impartial hearing before the school board, I could request a hearing conducted by the Division of Administrative Hearings of Florida's Department of Management Services.

If I had been teaching at the University of Central Florida or another of the state's universities and had been charged with wrongdoing, after exhausting internal procedures my case would have gone directly to a state hearing officer unconnected with the institution.

Forget those safeguards for Florida's community college faculties. I was on trial, and the trustees were judge and jury, the court of first and last resort. My fate rested with five pro-administration political appointees, all of whom had been bombarded with negative information about me from a half-dozen administrators. And not one of those trustees had ever exchanged a single word with me or, as far as I know, with other faculty about any of the dozens of issues involved. That my case would be heard before a kangaroo court was apparent.

First, there was a total disregard of the option of transferring me or pursuing any other of a dozen possible courses of action. Second, there was the obvious evidence of groundwork for my firing being laid at board meetings. Third, trustees Frank Williams and John Henry Jones

recused themselves. Their official presence during the
1990 May Massacre would have made it a cinch to establish trustee bias, thereby contaminating the whole procedure. Fourth, Simpkins wasn't admitting that he was, in
fact, in the audience during the May Massacre. (His term
of office officially began just two days later, so his appointment was already a done deal.) Fifth, the three remaining trustees—despite their presence in board meetings at which I had been thoroughly criticized by the administration, refused to recuse themselves. Sixth, those
same trustees—despite claims of being so busy that the
hearing worked a real hardship on them—steadfastly refused my lawyers' repeated motions that their hearing of
the case was not appropriate and that a state hearing officer should be requested.

No siree. No one was taking a chance on the conclusions of a neutral judge. The verdict was, then, absolutely
predictable.

Before the kangaroo court could convene, however, a
decision had to be made about what to do with me until
the administration's version of due process had run its
course. The fall 1992 term was about to start and I was
still on the payroll.

I hadn't yet had a hearing, but from King's perspective that was irrelevant. Knowing in advance the outcome, no classes for me to teach had been scheduled.
Instead, I was put in what amounted to solitary confinement. Day-to-day responsibility for me was given to Provost Tace Crouse.

Part of an article in the faculty newsletter described
my situation:

> This fall, Professor Brady disappeared. He has
> become a political prisoner. Provost Tace Crouse
> of the Cocoa campus to be his warden—the same
> Tace Crouse who is also named in the UFF law-

suit. Even though Professor Brady has been denied due process and is guilty of nothing except being accused by McCrory's trumped-up allegations, he has been assigned to an unused "office" in an obscure building in a seldom visited outback of the Cocoa campus where he has few neighbors. He is not permitted to teach classes. He may not go to the library. Someone else determines when he is allowed to eat. Crouse has exiled Brady to a windowless cell, musty and austere. He has been denied a telephone (the phone hookup has been hidden behind ceiling tile). His name doesn't even appear in the new college-wide Directory; he's been officially deleted.

Meanwhile, King, McCrory, Crouse, and even the Board of Trustees—their tax supported lawyers riding shotgun—are circling the wagons, denying that they have in any way violated Professor Brady's civil and First Amendment rights of free speech and association.

The situation is clearly out of control. The accused have been put in charge of the jail, and their accuser is their prisoner.

(Update, 9-92)

Had I written the article, I would have added another indignity: Crouse had all my mail delivered to her office.

If there was any doubt that my treatment was absolutely vindictive, it was removed when I discovered that two doors away from my "office" was a real office. It was carpeted, and contained a desk, swivel chair, four upholstered occasional chairs, a filing cabinet, two large bookshelves, and a working telephone. This office was empty during my entire confinement.

For almost seven months I spent my work day in isolation. Most faculty were so fearful of administrative wrath they wouldn't come to see me, and those who did usually stood in the doorway so they could duck away if they heard footsteps on the stairs.

I didn't spend much of my imprisonment thinking about what lay ahead. Since I already knew how it was all going to end, I was mostly curious about the procedure. I had one extremely vivid memory of such a hearing, and every time I thought about it, I oscillated between anger at the injustice of it, and being appalled that what I saw could take place in America.

Years before, back in the early '80's, faculty member Bill Wenz had taken the outrageous position that faculty ought to be allowed to appear before the trustees. The administration then proceeded to fabricate a case against him, using its anonymous-student-complaint tactic.

At the time of Wenz's hearing I was neither very knowledgeable about nor much interested in matters having to do with faculty-administration conflicts. I'm not even sure I was as yet a member of the union. But late one afternoon I went by the board room to listen and watch the proceedings.

The image of Wenz's hearing etched in my memory was this: A witness in his defense was testifying at a podium in front of and facing the five trustees. Whoever was testifying was talking directly to them.

Or at least trying to talk to them. One of the trustee chairs was empty—perhaps the trustee had gone to the bathroom. Trustee Palmer Collins was there, but he wasn't listening, he was talking. And he wasn't talking to the witness, or about the witness to counsel, or about anything having to do with the witness or the case. He was talking to King and laughing, loudly enough for me to hear him from my seat halfway back in the room. The topic of conversation? Whether or not they were all going to dinner afterwards, if so, where, and who would pick up the tab. All this in good fun, while Wenz's career hung in the balance. The witness might as well have been reciting nursery rhymes for all the difference it made.

I could have been wrong, but I recall thinking at the time that the point of the display was deliberate—to let King know that the whole exercise wasn't being taken seriously by the trustees.

"GROSS INSUBORDINATION"

Considering that my hearing lasted six days and generated 1,700 pages of official transcript, it's remarkable how little of it sticks in my memory.

I can only attribute that to my conviction that it didn't make any difference. Going into the proceedings, the trustees' intent was clear. If I had had some hope of the testimony turning them around, it didn't last past the first day. Simpkins, in the role of presiding judge, routinely overruled Brooks' and Chamblee's objections and sustained those of Jesse Hogg, the administration's attorney. Off and on, Rachel Moehle dozed off. Only Patrick Healy gave at least the appearance of trying to be objective, and a minority of one—even if he could see what was really going on (and I suspect that he could)—wasn't going to change the outcome.

Chamblee began the proceedings by laying out clear legal explanations of why the trustees were unqualified by reason of prior involvement to hear my case. All the trustees, he said, were in fact important material witnesses, and "if you have to testify, you can't sit in judgment on your own testimony."

HEALY: You want to call us to determine what occurred at that meeting that you have a transcript of?

CHAMBLEE: I want to know what information was received by the Board members, not just at the meeting [March 31 trustee meeting], but what occurred, what has been received by the Board members with respect to that meeting, which issues which were the subject of the Petition have already come to the Board members' attention . . .

I'm entitled to find out—it will happen in the Federal proceeding, if not now, whether or not the Board members were aware of the information contained in the proceeding . . .

(Brady Hearing transcript, p. 29)

The conclusion of the matter is recorded on pages 60 and 61 of the hearing transcript:

SIMPKINS: Mr. Healy, do you feel there's any reason that we are disqualified?
HEALY: No.
SIMPKINS: Mrs. Moehle, do you feel there's any reason we're disqualified?
MOEHLE: No.
SIMPKINS: Neither do I. So we unanimously agree that the hearing shall proceed on the basis of us hearing the case.

As if to underline the incredible irregularity of the entire proceeding, Hogg then said that he wanted to amend King's petition to fire me. He wanted permission to use against me not only the actions for which I was being charged, but my actions following the charges, actions for which I had never been charged and therefore had no prepared defense. This "sliding indictment" was to apply right up to that very moment.

> CHAMBLEE: Excuse me, can I be heard on this or am I sort of irrelevant to this hearing, which I kind of gathered to begin with?
>
> SIMPKINS: Just have a seat and we'll call on you to hear you in just a second, Mr. Chamblee. Are you through, Mr. Hogg?
>
> HOGG: I'm through, Mr. Chairman.
>
> SIMPKINS: Mr. Chamblee.
>
> CHAMBLEE: I've never heard of such a thing. I mean, is it appropriate that we just get up and leave and let y'all go ahead and do what you're going to do anyway?
>
> *(Brady Hearing transcript, pp. 62-63)*

We didn't leave, but we might as well have. It was a lost cause, but Chamblee didn't want anyone to forget what the real issue was:

> CHAMBLEE: What happens in between the time that Ann Thomas is the supervisor and Mr. McCrory becomes the supervisor is one thing and one thing only. And that is that this man right here wrote articles that appeared in *Florida Today*, wrote articles that appeared on campus, wrote articles that appeared before this Board, wrote articles or made correspondence which appeared before agencies stating his opinion about various matters and Maxwell King didn't like it. And Maxwell King said he didn't like it . . .

What Ann Thomas has testified to in her deposition is that she was confronted by at least two
administrators, Marquess and Purga, and told,
"Well, you need to take a close look at anybody
whose name appears in some communication
which has found its way outside the BCC community."

... The bottom line is that when Steve
McCrory came on board he had an instruction as
a result of what had happened to Ann Thomas,
and that instruction, that direction was that what
he needed to do was to pay close attention to this
man Marion Brady.

(Brady Hearing transcript, pp. 78-81)

Chamblee then walked through McCrory's "close attention," pointing out how differently he dealt with me
than with other faculty; how a single incident—my refusal
to meet with McCrory unless Aitken was present—was
made to appear as if it was several different incidents;
how McCrory's testimony and his deposition differed; how
clear it was that McCrory was, in fact, no longer my dean
after March 5 but continued to stuff my file; how the
whole procedure was purely and simply a vendetta
against me.

Chamblee reminded the trustees that I'd worked for
BCC for 15 years, under two other deans, who not only
hadn't had any problems with me, but considered me
"first rate."

The hearing proceeded: September 17, 18, 23, 24, and
October 6. I spent 11 hours on the stand, most of it
answering questions posed by Hogg that seemed to me to
be designed to establish that I was driven by racism,
jealousy, frustration or other reprehensible motives.

Kathy Tickner, Shawn Smith, Jeff Reynolds, Tom Ward, Julia Brooks, Anna Cate Blackmon, Jeff Neill, Linda Parrish, Jeff Johnson, Henry Carrier, Melissa Prevatt and Connie Bradish volunteered to testify on my behalf—faculty or staff with 10, 15, 20, 25 years of unblemished service to BCC. I can't imagine that any objective hearer of their testimony about me or events relative to my dismissal would have found it anything other than clear, unequivocal and straightforward. Other faculty also volunteered, but Hogg said their testimony wasn't necessary, that we'd adequately established our positions.

I won't comment about witnesses called by King, except to note that they were primarily administrators, newly appointed department heads, or faculty without tenure. They were vulnerable. Anyone who believed that a BCC administrator was free to tell the truth should have kept in mind one of King's early statements to administrators: "I serve at the pleasure of the board; you serve at my pleasure."

My doodled tally during King's relatively brief appearance on the stand indicated 20-plus repetitions of some variation of "I can't recall," and "I learned about that long after the fact."

In fact, he claimed to know so little about the petition for my dismissal—a document he had signed—that at the conclusion of his testimony Chamblee again moved that the Petition be dismissed on the grounds that the Petition was never "properly made by the person who's required to make it."

On March 18, 1993, I was officially fired for "gross insubordination." When the Final Order was drafted by Hogg for the signatures of the trustees, the additional original charges of "misconduct in office" were slipped back in. Chamblee caught the move and required that the order be changed to reflect the board's decision.

The three sitting trustees voted to pay me my accumulated sick leave worth about $13,000. The full board, at their next meeting, voted not to pay it.

I applied for unemployment compensation—the first time I had done so in a working career spanning 50 years. The College brought in their team of lawyers to fight it and, as of this writing, the matter was in litigation.

FLORIDA TODAY

Thomas Jefferson, in a 1787 letter to Colonel Edward Carrington, wrote, "Were it left to me to decide whether we should have a government without newspapers, or newspapers without government, I should not hesitate a moment to prefer the latter."

Given what appears to be human nature, one of the few defenses against abuses of power by those in positions of authority is the fear of exposure. In a mass and mobile society such as ours, the media carries a heavy responsibility for exposing official wrongdoing.

In Brevard County, "the media" was primarily the newspaper *Florida Today*.

I was never able to figure out where *Florida Today* was coming from. An incident that took place several years ago may be revealing.

I had asked for and gotten an appointment with *Florida Today*'s publisher, Frank Vega. We met in his big corner office in the Gannett complex on U.S. 1 north of Melbourne. In the course of our conversation about matters at the College, Vega referred to King as that "egotistical son of a bitch," said that he couldn't stand King's orchestrated congratulations of himself at just about every meeting, and then told me that he had resigned from the BCC Foundation's board of directors because he "couldn't afford to be associated with an operation like that."

I didn't know what he meant by "an operation like that," and I didn't feel at the time that it was appropriate to ask. However, there in a nutshell was much of my experience with *Florida Today*: a one-on-one conversation that dealt with a serious, surely newsworthy matter—serious enough to cause Vega to go to the trouble of resigning from BCC's Foundation, yet nothing except laudatory articles about BCC's Foundation ever appeared in the pages of the paper.

I had a fat file of correspondence to *Florida Today*'s publishers, executive editors, managing editors, editorial editors, metro editors, special features editors, columnists and reporters. I had written countless notes and memos. I had called these people so often I knew most of their numbers from memory. I had met with the paper's full editorial board and with many individuals. Sensitive to the fact that my tenacity was increasingly alienating at least some of the paper's personnel, I asked other, "cooler" people to speak to matters concerning the College.

But nothing happened. At one time, a large delegation of faculty met with the editorial board, and came away convinced that a major break was imminent. Much later, a "balanced" feature story on King appeared. Sometimes there were promises of investigations to come. Mostly there were explanations: "We can't afford investigative reporting." "Brevard's public school news is all we have time to cover." "We'll be getting around to BCC soon." "We're working on a really big, comprehensive story about BCC's administration." "I called that lead that you gave me but no one answered the phone." "We can't do a story because we can't get people to talk on the record."

Every time I'd hear one of those reasons, I'd think back to my days of teaching adolescents and the many

variations I'd heard of "The dog ate my homework."
When Glenda Busick's book, *Brevard's Good Ole Boys,*
came out with such an impact on local politics, I wrote a
note to a couple of people at the paper asking them if
they weren't embarrassed by the book's success, and its
obvious message that Brevard's citizens were hungry for
what they perceived as the real story.

Theories about *Florida Today* abounded among faculty: The paper's afraid of being sued. They're afraid of
losing advertising revenue. Their idea of an investigation
is to call Jim Ross, the College's public relations officer.
They're tied in to the local power structure. They're just
lazy. Their reporters are young, naive and not up to the
task. King has them totally snowed. It's Al Neuharth.
It's Malcolm Kirschenbaum. It's Guy Spearman. And so
on.

Executive Editor Ken Paulsen, and his successor,
Bennie Ivory, steadfastly insisted that the paper was
independent. Perhaps. But how could they explain that
not a **single** lead provided them had ever resulted in a
story? Why, for starters—considering the extent of the
documentation I had given them—had they done nothing
at all to look into the College's violations of the Fair
Labor Standards Act?

I just couldn't believe that Brevard's citizens wouldn't
be interested in knowing more about some of the ways in
which their money was being spent at the College. All I
asked was that the stories be checked out. If that had
been done, and *Florida Today* had come back to me three
or four times and told me that they had checked my
informants out and they were all wet, I'd have backed off
from sheer embarrassment.

Here are matters I thought readers would find interesting:

■ I, of course, gave *Florida Today* Russ Jones' letter
about his catering of King's private functions at public

expense, signing blank vouchers, bid padding and all the rest, and I told them that he had said there was more information where that came from. (I also gave Jones' letter to the *North Brevard Observer*, which printed major portions of it without, as far as I know, King attempting or even threatening a suit.)

■ Following a lead from Alan Thornquest and a lengthy discussion with an informant who called me one night, I told the paper about the possibility of some sort of secret deal between Minolta and BCC. The note I gave *Florida Today* suggested some very specific questions: Why are we building another planetarium when we've already got a good one? Did the starball that's presently stored in a crate on the second floor of the planetarium cost $1 million or $2 million? If we own the starball, how was it paid for, and why are there no College property tags on it? If we don't own it, what does Minolta expect in return for letting us use it? Are they just being nice? If so, how is it they decided to donate this world-class piece of equipment to us instead of a university in a metropolitan center somewhere? Does Minolta expect some kind of quid pro quo? If so, for a public institution, doesn't that get complicated?

And how about that "870" projector up there on the second floor keeping the starball company? Are we talking another half million dollars? More? Less? And again: Who does it belong to, how was it paid for, and if it's ours, why doesn't it have a College property tag on it? If it's not ours, whose is it?

And why, if this is a public institution, is no one allowed on the second floor of the planetarium? And why are employees constantly reminded to talk to no one about what they're doing, to direct all questions to the planetarium director?

And why does the planetarium have a staff of eight to ten full-time employees plus part-timers? What size student load are they carrying? (I even suggested that a story might explore the fact that the planetarium had many expensive full-time employees for a program that taught no students at all, while the Melbourne campus didn't even have a single full-time American history teacher.)

■ I passed along to *Florida Today* some fairly detailed information about a man named Jerry Wilborn, who did work for BCC under two different accounts, one under his name and the other under Wilborn Masonry. I told them that several past and present BCC employees believed that Wilborn was doubling the amount of hours required for work done for the College, and that he had done the slab, driveway and seawall for Vice President for Maintenance Harold Creel's house on Lake Poinsett as part of a kickback. I also gave them copies of two invoices—one dated 10-23-91 for $4,500, another dated 11-12-91 for $5,820—which suggested very strongly that the eight concrete footbridges on the Melbourne campus were bid separately. A reputable contractor I had look at the bridges said he'd build them forever for $1,400 apiece.

And, I was told, Wilborn helped himself to gasoline from BCC's private pump.

■ I told them that other college employees were saying that auto and truck parts were being purchased from Cocoa Motor Parts and Watson Motor Parts for use on privately owned vehicles and airboats—not just occasionally but constantly and routinely—on open accounts; that an outfit run by someone named Lacourt might somehow be involved, and that I had heard from several sources that Head College Mechanic Harold Grounds, under orders from Creel, was falsifying the paperwork. I also suggested they might check with the head of the police academy who, I'd heard, had doubts about work for which the Academy was charged actually having been done.

■ I told them that Leon Stearns, a retired BCC employee rehired as "Clerk of the Works," may have been sub-contracting landscaping and sprinkling system work on both the Melbourne and Cocoa campuses, work for which he was supposed to be the College's inspector. He was, I was told, using a Cocoa Beach friend as a front. For background, I told the paper that *Today* files would show that the newspaper's reporters had caught him several years before using college heavy equipment on his private property.

■ I wondered if there was any truth to the rumor that the original plans for the performing arts center called for an elevator for the handicapped, that it was deleted, and that a separate contract for its construction was subsequently given to a relative of King at a much higher cost.

■ When a couple of *Florida Today*'s satellite papers printed a picture of the president of Barnett Bank presenting $25,000 in scholarship money to King, I sent the paper a photocopy of a student loan application picked up at the student aid office on BCC's Melbourne campus. The form was pre-stamped to show Barnett Bank as the lender. I told the reporter that it was my understanding that student loan application forms were supposed to be blank, that it was up to borrowers to decide what institution they wished to use. Perhaps I was wrong, but maybe they'd like to check the matter out?

■ Early in 1993, I heard a rumor that BCC was going to auction off five brand new but out-of-date motorcycles donated to the College for instructional purposes by Honda. I gave *Florida Today* a complete package of documents—copies of BCC's contract with Honda saying that, if disposed of, the motorcycles had to be sold for scrap; documents showing that four of the bikes were sold without the permission of the trustees; documents showing who bought them, and a letter from Vice President Megregian falsely claiming that copies of the titles couldn't be produced because they had been given to the buyers. In fact, the College had never had titles. Honda hadn't provided them because their agreement with the College said the bikes were never to be ridden. In violation of state law, the College had sold motor vehicles without titles.

And I told the paper that my informants were saying that the real reason the motorcycles were stored for years and then illegally sold was because Vice President Creel wanted one of them, and that one of the two bikes purchased by Dencil's Used Cars was actually his.

■ I gave the paper detailed information about two different parties who had established scholarships with BCC's Foundation, and then were constantly put off when they asked for information. The donors couldn't find out about the recipients of the scholarships, and they couldn't get verification that the funds they donated were, in fact, matched 60%/40% as they had been promised. One of the two parties was so unhappy they wrote to BCC's Foundation asking for their $16,500 back, and saying, "We will redirect this to another fund which is more appreciative. We have also removed BCC Foundation from our wills. It could have benefitted by half a million dollars. We can imagine what could happen when we have passed on, and there is no one to check on our scholarships with the BCC Foundation. We are still here, and it is difficult."

■ Finally, realizing that information coming from me was heavily discounted by *Florida Today*, I offered names and telephone numbers of ex-BCC employees who told me they were willing to talk on the record about illegal actions of which they had direct knowledge. No one at *Florida Today* was interested.

I had all kinds of questions about the Foundation I thought the public had a right to have answered: Were the taxpayers, via the College, picking up the Foundation's operating expenses? What percentage of monies to "help students" actually went for student aid, and how much went for parties and other perks for Foundation members? (In one case I knew about, the College had employees produce a video tape to celebrate a Foundation member's birthday, and I was told that attendees at Foundation social functions were often given free photos of themselves courtesy of BCC's staff photographer.) Did the Foundation have a paid lobbyist? If so, why? What was the status of monies collected for "endowed faculty chairs" to which faculty contributed and heard nothing more? How blurred were the lines between the Foundation and the College? What kind of access did King have to Foundation monies? No doubt Foundations were legal, but were *any* non-student-oriented Foundation expenditures ethically defensible?

The Palm Beach Post fought lengthy court battles to get this kind of information from Ed Eissey, president of Palm Beach Community College. *Florida Today*, as far as I know, never so much as picked up the telephone to inquire about the operation of BCC's Foundation.

Those matters were just a beginning. Over the years, from maintenance workers, security personnel, secretaries, ex-employees and private citizens, came scores of bits of information that I passed along to *Florida Today*, information about sexual harassment, nepotism, illegal use of Staff and Program Development funds, intimidation of students, private businesses operating out of the College using College tools and materials, surplus government aircraft engines being obtained through the College and then used on airboats built for private sale, failure to investigate reported thefts by administrators, private use of College building materials, letting contracts to relatives, strong-arming lower-level administrators for political contributions, changing student grades without the knowledge of teachers, creating new, unneeded positions for friends and political allies, allowing the bookstore to charge excessively high prices, requiring that student loan monies be spent in the bookstore, routinely and frequently changing budget categories without notifying the affected departments, failing to discipline administrators caught in illegal or unethical actions, sending College employees out to work on non-College jobs, and requiring employees to sign open invoices.

Orlando Sentinel columnist Allen Rose, on the other hand, called them as he saw them—or at least did until the *Sentinel* editor knuckled under to a threat of legal action by King. Fred Krupske, editor of the *North Brevard News Observer*, also took some shots at the BCC administration. Perhaps I've forgotten, but I can't recall a single instance of a lead I gave *Florida Today* being investigated. Maybe they did but didn't tell me.

THE FDLE

When Melinda Meers came to *Florida Today* as its new managing editor in January of 1993, a newspaper insider told me that she had a reputation for digging up hard news. The opinion was seconded by a friend in Tallahassee who had edited a couple of the state's major newspapers.

At their suggestion, I went to see her, taking with me Russ Jones' letter, copies of student loan applications pre-stamped "Barnett Bank," detailed information about Wilborn Masonry, and a complete file on BCC's illegal sale of the five Honda motorcycles. I saw these as easy stories, stories that could be written after little more than a few telephone calls.

She promised to look into the matters.

In the weeks that followed, after two or three unanswered faxes and a couple of phone conversations, it became clear that it was business as usual at the paper. Frustrated, I called my friend in Tallahassee.

He told me to send some of my material to him, and he'd see that it got attention as soon as the current legislative session was over.

I sent him seven numbered packages of information and waited to see what, if anything, would happen.

I heard no more about it until Tuesday morning, the 26th of July.

A little after seven o'clock on the evening of June 20, there was a knock at my door. A young man who had been employed by BCC for about four and a half years introduced himself and said he had some things I might like to see.

He was right. For the next two hours, he showed me documents, talked about specific incidents at the College of which he had knowledge, and expressed extreme frustration that what he felt were flagrant violations of law could continue year after year without consequences.

He had a great deal of information, and a willingness to testify about what he knew. He provided details about matters of which I had only general information, told me much that I hadn't heard before, and gave me a list of people he thought should be called to testify under oath about the operation of the College's maintenance department.

Since, I hope, the matters about which he talked will eventually result in indictments, I'll note only that he discussed many matters, including kickback procedures, parts and equipment paid for by the College but diverted to private use, and the relationships between various College employees and outside contractors.

His information seemed to me to warrant immediate action. I called the Florida Department of Law Enforcement in Tallahassee, arranged a meeting, drove to Tallahassee the evening of the 25th of July, and met with FDLE Investigator T.W. Smart the next morning.

Smart turned on a tape recorder at about 10 o'clock, swore me in, and we talked until almost lunch time. At the conclusion of my testimony, he shut the tape recorder off, told me that I had convinced him that there were, in fact, serious problems at the College, and said that, since I had shared a stack of documents with him, he would share some with me.

"Great," I thought to myself, "If there's a file, they must be working on it."

What he had, as it turned out, was the seven packages of material I had earlier sent to my Tallahassee friend, plus a couple of letters and a report. Smart asked me if I'd take the material home and respond to it.

I stopped in Williston to get a sandwich, and took what he'd given me into the restaurant to read while I ate.

What I read didn't do much for my appetite. About three bites into my sandwich I learned that the FDLE investigator, instead of initiating an investigation, had simply sent all my material to Sydney McKenzie, General Counsel for the State Board of Community Colleges. (The SBCC, remember, is the organization that, when we tried to get them to investigate the matter of BCC equipment being used off campus to manufacture airboats, refused, telling us, "We're just family, you know.")

McKenzie, in turn, had sent the material to Max King. My entire package of evidence had been handed over to the accused! I could hardly believe it.

But that wasn't the end of it. King had given the package to Jim Ross, BCC's Administrative Director of College Relations, to investigate. Ross's "investigation" had then been accepted by McKenzie, and then by the FDLE, as a sufficient basis for closing the case.

I spent the rest of the evening writing a critique of "Chief Inspector" Ross's report, and faxed it to Smart the next morning. Its five pages are too long to reproduce, so I'll summarize.

I told Smart that I'd deal with every one of Ross's excuses and rationalizations, but I had three or four observations that I wanted to make first.

I told him what a serious mistake I thought it was for the FDLE to have pursued a course of action that resulted in the actual documents I had sent ending up in the hands of Brevard Community College administrators. Some of those documents, I pointed out, could only have come from perhaps as few as two people. By circulating them, those individuals were put in great danger of losing their jobs. In fact, I said, I was surprised that that hadn't already happened.

Second, I reminded him that when I initially approached the local FDLE investigator about investigating BCC administrators, that investigator had begun by calling BCC administrators on the telephone. For all practical purposes, I told him, that approach had now been repeated. In both instances, closure had come on the basis of an assurance by BCC administrators that the charges were baseless—the rantings of a disgruntled faculty member. For the life of me, I said, I couldn't understand how an investigation that began by asking the accused if they were guilty, and ended by accepting at face value their assurance that they were not, could be defended.

Third, I told him that forwarding specific documents to the accused seemed to me to be an open invitation to destroy important evidence.

I also commented about the cover letter from King to the State Board of Community College's General Counsel, Sydney McKenzie:

> I'm sure you'll recall some of my comments about first-hand evidence of a good-ole-boy network that seems in part responsible for the failure of watchdog agencies to investigate the BCC administration. In light of those comments, should I not at least note that King's letter to McKenzie

begins, "Dear Sid," and is signed, "Max"? Granted, that doesn't prove a thing, but does it not suggest at least the possibility that there exists a
close and long-standing relationship that could get
in the way of McKenzie's objective consideration
of evidence?

I wish space permitted a complete reprinting of Ross's
report to King of his "investigation" of my charges. By
his own testimony, he discussed the material only with
those individuals who stood accused by the material itself, and accepted from them explanations that proved
nothing at all except his apparent naiveté.

Of the Barnett Bank matter, Ross said that the reason the College could produce only student loan forms
pre-stamped with the name of that bank was "because on
a temporary basis [other] bank forms are out and we are
awaiting more."

About the Honda motorcycles, he referred to the
"three motorcycles," (there were five), ignored the contract with Honda that said the motorcycles could be sold
only for scrap to be crushed or melted down, said that
board permission to sell them wasn't necessary because
only one was valued at over $500, and then made no at-
tempt whatsoever to explain why the auction report said
that, although one of the bikes actually did sell for $450
and another for $500, a third sold for $1,750, a fourth for
$2,000, and the fifth for $2,200. He also made no mention
of whether or not BCC Vice President Creel ended up
with the pick of the litter.

Ross dealt with the Wilborn Masonry material primarily by insisting that Dane Construction had made
more money from the College during the past year than
Wilborn. He also maintained that the copies of invoices
that I had for two of the eight concrete footbridges on the
Melbourne campus covered the cost of all of them. He

made no attempt to explain why one of the invoices for approximately $5,000 included the wording, "One only."

I had included a copy of the Russ Jones letter. Ross made no mention of it at all in his report.

The fifth item I had sent dealt with BCC's Foundation, and the frustrating experience of contributors when they attempted to find out what had happened to their money. Ross had nothing to say on this subject either.

Item six in the package was a copy of "Priorities," the booklet with twelve pages of questions from faculty and staff about College operations. Again, Ross had nothing to say.

The seventh matter had to do with College employee Virgil Fulford's personal use of College equipment and materials. Once again, Ross was silent.

Finally, I had included in my original submission a brief account of a conversation my brother had with Gene Lye, the owner of a couple of local music stores. Lye alleged that College administrator Bill Baker had disregarded the only two bids submitted for an organ for the College and bought one from a third party who hadn't even participated in the bid process.

I said:

> As for the organ question, Ross's explanation sounds superficially plausible. An investigator should show it to Lye and the other bidder and get their reactions. I would, however, really like to know more about those organs. If not buying Lye's organ saved the College "several thousand dollars," and the other one cost so little that "the price did not require a bid process," this is surely the deal of the century. That [second] organ must be a dandy.

I had opened the critique of Ross's report by noting that Ross's primary job at the College was to write promotional puff pieces, and asking how that could possibly qualify him to investigate charges of criminal behavior. I ended it with some general observations:

> I'll have to say that, after reading the material you gave me, I'm appalled that [the State Board of Community Colleges and the Florida Department of Law Enforcement] considered it an adequate basis for closure of the case . . . The amateurishness of the "investigator," his vested interest in finding nothing wrong (he wrote it for his accused boss), the document's shrill tone, the constant use of hyperbole, the obvious internal inconsistencies, the reliance on the testimony of the accused, the implausibility of many of the claims—it's all just too much.

I'd like to say that the FDLE jumped back into the matter. That didn't happen. They told me that, because my information was "secondhanded," they weren't going to look into it. They would, however, forward my material to the State's Comptroller, and would get involved if their investigation warranted it.

As of early fall, 1994, that's how it stood.

Reviewing the material I had sent to the FDLE—the student loan application clearly stamped "Barnett Bank," the detailed paper trail for the illegal sale of the motorcycles, the twelve pages of unanswered faculty and staff questions in "Priorities," the Russ Jones letter, and all the rest—the "secondhand" label just didn't fit. Add to that the acceptance of Jim Ross's amateurish sleuthing. I had difficulty avoiding the conclusion that the Florida Department of Law Enforcement and the State

Board of Community Colleges had just demonstrated for me how a cover-up works.

But why? I don't know. However, I recall that several years ago I stood in the lobby of a Cocoa Beach motel and watched lower- and middle-level BCC administrators drop personal checks into a punch bowl as contributions to a member of Florida's cabinet. Maybe there's a connection.

Note: In Ross's report to King, he said he'd spent 100 hours of College time and 40 hours of his own time on his investigation. The more I thought about it, the more incredible his claim seemed. One hundred forty hours—the equivalent of almost a month of full-time work—must have produced a small mountain of paper.

I wanted to see that mountain, as was my right under Florida Statute 119. So did Attorney Bill Horner. Horner put in his first request for it on the 29th of September, 1994. Over the next three months, he repeated his request more than a dozen times. Eventually, he went to the State Attorney's office to ask that they initiate action against King for failing to comply with Florida's "government in the sunshine" laws.

I wrote a letter to King with my own request for Ross's material on the 26th of October, and again on the 31st, and sent copies of both to the State Attorney's office and the appropriate officials in Tallahassee.

When this manuscript went to press in the middle of November, neither Horner nor I had received so much as a single page of the supporting documentation Ross said he had collected. And the State Attorney's office had, without explanation, declined to act.

Questions occur. Does the documentation supporting Ross's conclusions actually exist? Would Ross raise his right hand and swear to that 140-hour figure, or was that another crude public relations ploy to try to paint me, once again, as a drag on taxpayers? What's with State Attorney Norm Wolfinger's office when it comes to dealing with the area's power structure? For years, believing those who said that that office wouldn't confront it, I'd taken allegations of felonious activity elsewhere. Was I now seeing, in my inability to even get an appointment with Wolfinger, evidence that my informants were right? Following the actions of the FDLE, the State Board of Community Colleges, the BCC administration and the State Attorney's office, could I conclude anything other than that laws were useless when those charged with enforcing them refused to do so?)

AFTERGLOW

"Lies, half-truths and innuendo," will almost certainly be Maxwell King's response to *Max & Me*, and legal action against me will probably be undertaken. (At taxpayer expense, of course.) But this isn't necessarily bad. I figure that the more he protests, the more people will read what I've had to say, and the more people who read what I've said, the more likely it is that the legislature will listen to Florida TaxWatch and the Post-Secondary Educational Planning Commission and close the door on the more flagrant, costly abuses of power by community college administrations.

In his defense, King will point to his "national reputation" to dazzle citizen bystanders who know little about real education and are impressed by vague claims and grandiose-sounding programs. He'll cite his "investigations," and maintain that all charges against him were, without exception, proven false. And he will point to state auditors' reports as proof that all is well, adding that the taxpayers have been the ones who have suffered from having to bear the cost of the investigation of my "baseless charges."

Self-investigations are, of course, worthless. State audits, however, are surely another matter.

Perhaps. I know almost nothing about audit procedures. However, I know that four state auditors once sat at my dining room table and said that the legislature had not provided them with adequate tools for thoroughly investigating community college finances. The situation was far different, they said, in Florida's K-12 and university systems.

I know also that, during the last audit, when maintenance department employees were asked to show auditors the actual parts on vehicles that their paperwork said had been installed, a witness said afterwards that the College had "gotten lucky," because Maintenance could produce on four of the five requests. On the fifth, the auditor bought the story that the truck he wanted to check was on another campus.

"If he had asked to see twenty items instead of five," they said, "the game would have been up."

Certainly some of what I've noted in *Max & Me* is a consequence of misperception. But I flatly reject the contention that all's well, that the King administration is squeaky clean and has nothing to hide.

First, it's inconceivable that a faculty and staff as large as that at BCC, on campus every day and with contacts reaching every corner of the institution, could be thoroughly misguided, wrongly believing that an administration was corrupt when, in fact, it was without blemish.

Second, too many of the reports of wrongdoing include details that make fabrication seem unlikely, even if there was some reason to make false accusations. A rumor that when the King Center was painted, paint was overbought by 125 gallons, and this excess was then traded to Gold Coast Building Supply for roofing materials for Vice President Creel's new house on Lake Poinsett, contains specific details that make it sound plausible. I have far more reason to trust the sources of my information than

I have reason to trust the denials of King, Megregian and Creel.

Third, there is the BCC administration's penchant for secrecy. Despite Florida's "government in the sunshine" laws, getting public records and other information requires maneuvering through a complex obstacle course, complete with constant queries of why certain information is being requested. For years, King fought the right of faculty and private citizens to address the trustees at all, even when they were in formal session, and tried to punish those who demanded the right. An administration with nothing to hide doesn't systematically block access to its paper trail.

Fourth, there are the dozens of silent witnesses to the King administration's intolerance of dissent—an honor roll of first-rate people forced out because they refused to knuckle under to an administration they considered crooked and inept. (One told me he could live with honest but inept, or dishonest but smart, but dishonest and inept together were more than he could bear.)

A paragraph from Section 402.02 of the College's policy manual makes clear King's attitude toward dissent (and the First Amendment):

> The president or designee will establish guidelines which will delineate types of acceptable dissent which might occur during the expression of free speech and dissent on College property. . . .

Fifth, there is my own personal experience—the years of being called on the carpet every time I wrote publicly about the College, the evasiveness of the administration when I raised questions about our foreign travel business, the string of misrepresentations of facts related to BCC violations of the Fair Labor Standards Act, the use of a hatchet man to put together an incredibly crude case against me that would have been laughed out of a proper court, the forged counterfeit memo that showed up during my hearing, the flat denials by administrators, under oath, of facts and events witnessed by scores of faculty of unquestioned character. And on and on.

Sixth, there was my firing. My charges against the administration could have been investigated. They weren't. The trustees could have talked to me one-on-one. They didn't. I could have been transferred to a different campus. My request was refused. The trustees could have allowed me to appear before a neutral State hearing officer. They wouldn't consider it. I could have been put on probation. I wasn't. My "insubordination" could have been put in perspective—put up alongside undisputed wrongdoing as recorded in newspaper accounts. There was, for example, Administrator Bill Baker's thousands of dollars worth of private abuse of the State's official phone system; Clerk of the Works Leon Stearns' personal use of College heavy equipment; the newspaper article saying that Administrator Johnny Walker had engaged in forcible, knife-point rape. These people were given gentle slaps or no penalties at all. I was fired.

Finally, even as I write, the stories continue. During the seventh and last week that I spent writing *Max & Me*, long-time BCC security guard Richard Parham told me that he saw BCC employee Virgil Fulford, one of the many Fulfords and Fulford relatives working for the College, routinely using a College truck for personal business. Virgil not only enjoyed the private use of a vehicle provided by taxpayers, he appeared to live free on College property, in a mobile home with direct access to the College's maintenance department, running a private air conditioning business.

Again: On the way to lunch at a Clearlake Road deli, I noted that a strip parallel to Clearlake in front of BCC's administration building had been graded. "A new sidewalk," I thought to myself, and I wondered if Wilborn was at it again.

A day or two later, some rather amateurish forms for a concrete pour suggested I might be right.

But then, the project stopped. The forms came out, and the land was regraded.

I asked a couple of sources what had happened. "They tried to pour a sidewalk without getting a permit," I was told. "Four thousand dollars for nothing."

Again: Lew Cresse, retired BCC history teacher who was put through King's wringer with particular ferocity several years ago, called me on a Friday afternoon to make small talk. I had written the last word of this manuscript and shut off the computer about 15 minutes earlier. He asked what I'd been doing. When I told him, and gave him the title of my manuscript, he asked me if I'd included the latest on nepotism.

"What's the latest?" I said.

"Well, as I understand it," he said, "Tace Crouse pushed someone named Helen Dezendorf out of her job at Cocoa's computer lab and made one of King's daughters Lab Coordinator. Dezendorf had a B.A. degree and was really knowledgeable about computers. King's daughter is really nice, but she just has an A.A. degree and the only thing she knows about computers is what she learned typing personal papers on WordPerfect."

I called Ms. Dezendorf. "Lew has it right," she said.

Again: In May of 1994, the weekly newspaper *The Brevard Reporter* carried a story merely reviewing my case. BCC canceled all advertising with the paper. When reporter Carole Hayes subsequently went to the College to obtain public records for a possible story on another matter, she got such a runaround from College officials that an account of the runaround itself became a story in the paper. That story, in turn, brought a letter from BCC carrying a not-so-subtle threat of libel action against the paper.

Really now, Judge Kellem. There's no basis for a case against BCC's administration?

NOW WHAT?

I'm no expert in institutional dynamics. However, there seem to me to be some rather obvious measures that could be taken to close off the valves through which unprincipled community college presidents are channeling wealth and power to themselves:

Presidency

■ Require community college presidents to undergo annual, publicly conducted performance reviews.
■ Eliminate "rolling," automatically renewing presidential contracts. Make them annual, like the university presidents' contracts.
■ Eliminate "golden parachutes" so that dumping a president doesn't cost the taxpayers a fortune.
■ Prohibit joint president-trustee and president-legislator business deals.

Money

■ Eliminate or drastically scale back community college public relations budgets.
■ Prohibit payment of public monies or foundation monies to community college lobbyists.
■ Put ownership of community college buildings in state hands.
■ Put all foundations under the Public Records Act umbrella.
■ Hand over all community college non-educational activity (performing arts centers, golf courses, dormitories, restaurants, liquor lounges, etc.) to the private sector. Alternatively, require that they be self-supporting, so that education

funds go for education. At a minimum, require
separate budgeting.

■ Adopt an absolutely uniform accounting
system that makes game playing with public
monies much more difficult.

Trustees

H.G. Wells once wrote, "Civilization is a race between
education and catastrophe." To put final authority for an
educational institution in the hands of a few people who
meet for an hour or so once a month, and whose primary
qualification for a trustee position is usually that they
contributed money to a gubernatorial candidate, is ludicrous. Major changes are called for.

■ Set up a state-wide nonpartisan screening
board to rate and recommend community college
trustee applicants.

■ Eliminate all community college administration influence in the trustee selection process.

■ Require six months advanced public notice
of prospective trustee candidates, with formal provision for public feedback to the governor on each
candidate.

■ Make clear to every community college
trustee that the contention that it's illegal for
them to talk to anyone excepting the college president because it interferes with the collective bargaining process is administrative propaganda. Tell
them that they have not only a right but a duty to
be open to all sources of information about the
institutions for which they are responsible, and
that if they think that they're getting the whole
story from the community college presidents, they
may have to pay a steep price for their naiveté.

Staffing

■ Establish appropriate teacher/administrator/staff ratios in line with national averages.
■ Prohibit hiring of family members of trustees and upper-echelon administrators.
■ Mandate the use of verifiable, competitive faculty and staff selection procedures.

Legal Action

■ Adopt K-12 due process procedures in actions against faculty charged with wrongdoing.
■ Put copies of ALL board minutes, addenda, etc. in readily accessible public locations.
■ Devise some system to level the legal-system playing field for ordinary people attacked by exploitative administrators.
■ Since the state pays most of the costs of community colleges, make community college workers employees of the state, with the attendant contracts.
■ If a community college official takes legal action against a critic or a whistleblower and loses, make him or her reimburse the taxpayers for all litigation costs.
■ Halt all attempts to abolish tenure. As long as community college administrators cling to 19th century conceptions of management, tenure will be necessary. When phrases such as "chain of command" and "insubordination" disappear from policy manuals, it may then be appropriate to discuss alternative faculty quality control measures.

Philosophy

■ In the long run, the most important (and the most difficult) community college reform requires abandonment of the military model of management that dominates the thinking of many administrators. Counterproductive authoritarian management styles are gradually being pushed aside in business and industry. Unfortunately, the market forces that drive reforms in those sectors are, in educational institutions, either absent or are too subtle to exert pressure for change.

Managerial success is rooted in organizational pride and enthusiasm for the task at hand. When presidents think their primary role is that of cop, spy, controller, nay sayer, judge, enforcer, or even benevolent parent, organizational pride and enthusiasm—and the quality that pride and enthusiasm foster—remain forever out of reach of everyone else in the organization.

This simple, common-sense notion, now the conventional wisdom in the private sector, has yet to be acknowledged on many community college campuses. The irony of it lies in the fact that, far more than in business and industry, college employees represent a collective level of expertise exceeding that of those who often order them around in such demeaning fashion.

This is the problem Florida's legislature must confront if institutional excellence is sought. It's an exceedingly difficult challenge. The situation that must be turned around was aptly described by management expert Warren Bennis: "American organizations have been overmanaged and underled."

None of the preceding suggestions is likely to seem reasonable to Florida's community college presidents. Even those who don't say, "It's my college, and I'll run it the way I damn well please," will nevertheless resist change. And their resistance will be formidable, for they're allied with trustees, paid lobbyists, contractors, developers, bankers and other special interests that benefit from the present system.

An excerpt from an August 1994 "Briefings" from Florida TaxWatch illustrates the difficulties.

Sen. James Hargrett, D-Tampa, filed a bill this year that would have fixed a lot of the problems pointed out by Florida TaxWatch, including the multi-year annual renewal contracts of community college presidents.

Sen. Hargrett would restrict continuing contracts to two years and make renewal of a community college president's contract subject to a formal evaluation that includes a number of considerations, such as resolution of employee grievances, efforts to collect student concerns, success in achieving accountability goals, success in graduating minorities and retention and graduation rates for degree-seeking students. The senator also would place a restriction on how much future annual leave could be accumulated. The Florida Tax-Watch report found that in May 1993, the potential cost to taxpayers of a president's accrued annual and sick leave was as high as $141,056 at one college.

The Hillsborough senator's bill was watered down, combined with another bill and bounced from committee to committee in 1994, but it never came to a vote in either the House or Senate.

Legislators who take on the community college presidents and the special interests that profit from the status quo will deserve the taxpayers' sincere gratitude for saving them millions of dollars and fighting for educational excellence in Florida's community colleges.

LCCC board attorney

Heimer wants lawyer fired after his probe into purchase of flawed computer sys...

LCCC interna

By ED K...

DBCC trustee questioned

By DONNA CALLEA
Daytona Beach News-Journal
DAYTONA BEACH—

type questions concer
the project

Heise goes before et

sure trips taken to the west

HCC president defends fu

Students provide the majority of revenue for social and promotional events that administrators, not students, attend.

By JIM SLOAN and IVAN J. HATHAWAY
Staff Writers
Tampa Tribune

TAMPA — A gourmet dinner, dances, floor shows, a $100-a-ticket reception for Barbara Bush and a luncheon with the Bucs.

These are some of the events Hillsborough Community College (HCC) President Andreas Paloumpis and his top administrators attended over the last two years, courtesy of a special hospitality and public relations fund called the President's Activity Fund.

The money comes from profits from the college store, vending machine and cafeteria sales, where the ...id mostly by students. Only $9,000 of $73,000 ...ent to a tivities

HCC public re
Here are some events Hills
President's Activity Fund has

■ Cocktails, hors d'oeuvres,
and dancing for HCC Presider
three administrators and th
Chamber of Commerce's Si
Columbia Restaurant in Sept

■ Monthly dues for two yea
in the Centre Club, a private

■ Two tables for Paloumpis,
and guests at the Greater Br
annual banquet and ball Jar

■ Tickets for Paloumpis an
1991 Meet the Bucs Lunchea

ants investigation

ditor resigns

f management since both hus-
deal with school financ-

out Four Townes center

s and disbursements for   helped DBCC attorney Dana Fogle put together the deal
was renamed the Fou   Townes project earlier this year, and then
                            when problems arose.

s panel Tuesday

to get a written
told

Chronology of charges against Heise

hronology of events
rrent state Ethics
es Indian River
ge   President

use

2:    Heise's
structed with
RCC workers.

efforts
community College
the last two years.

State Attor-
th Judicial Cir-
stigate allega-
personnel and
s Fort Pierce

dinner, floor show
Paloumpis, his wife,
at the Ybor City
rsary Gala at the
0.
Cost: $400

: The staff of
wned public
publicly that
he station's

mpis' membership
b.
Cost: $1,537

Heise fires
ager   Brian
causing the
y. He rehires
t day, after re-

16 adiministrators
mber of Commerce
Hyatt Regency.
Cost: $1,000

ministrators to
yatt Regen
that his "abrasive personality"
was causing.

, 1983: Heise fires
again because of prob-
ms that his "abrasive personality"

■ **Sept. 12, 1985:** The Ethics
Commission releases the report of
an investigation outlining charges
related to construction of Heise's
Fort Pierce home.

■ **Nov. 5, 1985:** Heise officially
deeds his Fort Pierce home to IRCC
Foundation.

■ **Jan. 21, 1986:** The Florida
Auditor General's Office criticizes
IRCC's accounting practices, questioning Heise's travel records in a
report of fiscal years 1981-82 and
1983-84.

■ **Feb. 11, 1986:** Schneider
files seven new allegations against
Heise, including one that he was
improperly reimbursed for personal
vacation expenses and that he failed
to file his position with a local bank
by a 1984 deadline.

■ **Feb. 20, 1986:** The Ethics
Commission rejects Heise's settlement proposal to drop charges related to the construction of his home
in exchange for a $500 reimburse-
ment of investigation charges and
materials.

■ **June 12, 1986:** The Ethics

PLAINTIFFS' EXHIBIT LIST • CASE NO. 92-709-CN-ORL-18
UNITED STATES DISTRICT COURT
MIDDLE DISTRICT OF FLORIDA • ORLANDO DIVISION

1. Letter to Maxwell C. King from Charlie Harris, President of Florida AFL-CIO, dated April 1, 1970
2. Letter to Maxwell C. King from David Selden, President AFT, dated April 2, 1970
3. Letter to Steven Valavanis from Maxwell C. King, dated April 29, 1970
4. Memorandum to Paul Wignall, Campus Representative, FAPJC from A. Perkins Marquess, re: Meeting times for Professional Organizations, dated September 16, 1970
5. Memorandum to John O'Shea, President of Faculty Senate from Maxwell King re: Senate Minutes of March 8, 1972 dated April 4, 1972
6. Letter to Palmer Collins from Lewis Cresse, dated August 19, 1975
7. Letter and attached Petition from PERC, dated September 22, 1975
8. Notice of Representation Hearing before PERC, dated October 28, 1975
9. Memorandum to Cocoa Campus Faculty from R.J. Kosiba re: Collective Bargaining, dated January 6, 1976
10. Memorandum to Faculty, Titusville Campus from William Nunn re: Collective Bargaining, dated January 6, 1976
11. Memorandum to Melbourne Campus Members of Designated Voting Unit from A. Perkins Marquess re: Collective Bargaining, dated January 6, 1976
12. Letter to Colleague from Maxwell King, dated February 27, 1976
13. For your information BCCFT comparing letter written by Peter Masiko, President of Miami-Dade and Maxwell King
14. Memorandum to All Teaching Faculty, Librarians and Counselors from Maxwell King re: Information concerning voting for or against collective bargaining on March 3, 1976, dated February 19, 1976
15. Letter to Colleague from Lew Cresse, President BCC Federation of Teachers
16. Letter and attached Unfair Labor Practice Charge to Lewis Cresse from PERC, dated April 13, 1976
17. Subpoena Duces Tecum for Lewis Cresse from PERC
18. Faculty Resolution dated December 2, 1980
19. Report and other documents relating to the Academic Due Process Committee for the grievance filed by Dr. Lewis Cresse (Composite)
20. Letter to Nicholas Rahal from James Humphrys re: no longer furnishing copies of the Board of Trustees personnel actions, dated March 3, 1980
21. Newspaper articles (Composite)
22. BCCFT Newsletters from September, 1975 to January, 1983 (Composite)
23. "PULSE" publications from December, 1980 to May, 1982 (Composite)
24. Letter to Board of Trustees from Brevard Community College Chapter of United Faculty of Florida, dated March 15, 1988
25. President's Blue Ribbon Committee, Management Process Subcommittee's Interim and Summary Reports (Composite)
26. Memorandum to Members, Board of Trustees from Maxwell King re: Response to Blue Ribbon Committee Recommendations, dated July 13, 1988
27. Pamphlet entitled "The Code of Ethics of the Education Profession in Florida and The Principles of Professional Conduct for the Education Profession in Florida"
28. Priorities
29. Mailing list (Composite)
30. Presentation to Trustees of Brevard Community College by James A. Hooper, dated February 15, 1989
31. Citizen Presentation to Board of Trustees by Val Batts, dated April 19, 1989
32. United Faculty of Florida Brevard Community College Faculty Survey, dated March, 1990
33. Letter to Mr. Williams from Kathleen Tickner, dated May 31, 1990
34. Letter to Trustees from Neil Hamilton, dated June 20, 1990

35. Letter from Russ Jones, dated July, 1990
36. Letter to Charles Lester, Auditor General from Maxwell King, dated August 30, 1990
37. Letter to Maxwell C. King from June England, dated November 26, 1990
38. Communiques from April, 1969 to March 5, 1992 (Composite)
39. UPDATEs from February, 1990 to June, 1992 (Composite)
40. Press Release Guide
41. Board of Trustees Brevard Community College Policy Manual
42. Operational Procedures Manual Brevard Community College
43. Brevard Community College Catalog (Composite)
44. Minutes of the Board of Trustees meeting on May 9, 1985
45. Minutes and tape recording of the Board of Trustees special meeting on May 30, 1990
46. Minutes of the Board of Trustees meeting on February 20, 1991
47. Minutes and tape recording of the Board of Trustees meeting on February 13, 1992
48. Minutes, tape recording and transcribed excerpts of the Board of Trustees meeting on March 12, 1992
49. Personnel Actions, dated March 12, 1992
50. Minutes, tape recording and transcribed excerpts of the Board of Trustees meeting on April 9, 1992
51. Minutes, tape recording and transcribed excerpts of the Board of Trustees meeting on May 14, 1992
52. Minutes and tape recording of the Board of Trustees meeting on June 11, 1992
53. Minutes and tape recording of the Board of Trustees meeting on June 29, 1992
54. Minutes, tape recording and transcribed excerpts of the Board of Trustees meeting on August 13, 1992
55. Minutes and tape recording of the Board of Trustees meeting on September 10, 1992
56. Memorandum to File from Bob Craig re: "Fresh Start Meeting"
57. Written statement of Alecia Elbert, dated July 2, 1992
58. Guest column by Maxwell King entitled "BCC management will continue to do what is right for the college"
59. Memorandum to Brady from McCrory, dated 11/15/91 re: Letter of Reprimand—Gross Insubordination
60. Memorandum to Brady from McCrory, dated 11/13/91 re: Scheduled Meeting
61. Karen Booth letter (undated)
62. Ansley Sliker letter (undated)
63. Composite—Memorandum to Lawton from McCrory, dated 11/18/91 re: Letter of Reprimand; Memorandum to Brady from McCrory re: Letter of Reprimand—Gross Insubordination
64. Memorandum to Brady from McCrory, dated 1/16/92 re: Rescheduled Meeting
65. Memorandum to Aitken from McCrory, dated 2/18/92 re: Faculty Recommendation 1992-93—Marion Brady
66. Interoffice Memorandum to McCrory from Carol Marx, dated 2/19/92 re: Conversation with Marion Brady with attached handwritten note to Marion from Carol
67. Memorandum to Aitken from McCrory, dated 2/21/92 re: Letter of Reprimand—Marion Brady with attached Memorandum to Brady from McCrory, dated 2/19/91 re: Letter of Reprimand—Neglect of Duty
68. Memorandum to Aitken from McCrory, dated 3/2/92 re: Mr. Marion Brady's 1991-1992 Evaluation
69. Administrative Performance Review of Instructional Faculty for Marion Brady, dated 12/20/91
70. Handwritten note from Brady, dated 2/28/92 with attached 5 pages in response to his evaluation

71. Memorandum to Brady from McCrory, dated 1/16/92 re: Letter of Reprimand—Non-Professionalism with attached letters from Booth and Sliker and Memo to Aitken from Brady, dated 1/13/92
72. Memorandum to Brady from McCrory, dated 5/17/92 re: Scheduled Meeting
73. Memorandum to Brady from McCrory, dated 5/29/92 re: Request for Administrative Action
74. Faculty Office Hours
75. Alternative Option to Faculty Office Hours
76. Memorandum to Jim Cole from Stevan McCrory re: Kathy Tickner Workload Schedule, dated February 12, 1992
77. Composite—Memo, dated April 14, 1992; Faculty Schedule; Memo, dated April 20, 1992; Handwritten note; Memo, dated April 20, 1992; Handwritten memo, dated May 12, 1992; Memo, dated May 20, 1992; Memo, dated May 21, 1992; Handwritten note by McCrory, dated May 20, 1992; Handwritten note; Memo, dated May 19, 1992; Memo, dated May 21, 1992; Memo, dated May 26, 1992
78. Memorandum re: counseling with Brady on October 28, 1991
79. Composite—Memo from McCrory, dated January 15, 1992; Memo from McCrory, dated March 3, 1992; Memo from McCrory, dated May 12, 1992; Memo from McCrory, dated May 13, 1992; Note to Peg, dated May 21, 1992; Grievance, signed June 15, 1992; Memo from McCrory, dated June 30, 1992; Memo from McCrory, dated May 28, 1992
80. Memo to Dr. Robert Aitken from Stevan McCrory re: Dismissal of Employee—Marion Brady, dated April 21, 1992
81. Agreement between the District Board of Trustees and United Faculty of Florida 1991-1994
82. Memo to Brady from McCrory re: Grievance dated May 5, 1992, dated May 18, 1992
83. Memorandum for Record from Stevan McCrory, dated April 15, 1992
84. Memo from McCrory, dated April 20, 1992
85. Grievance filed by Marion Brady, dated April 21, 1992
86. Faculty Development Program Procedures
87. Audit Report for fiscal year ending June 30, 1991
88. Memorandum of record by Tace Crouse, dated September 16, 1992
89. Academic Management Team minutes 7/25/90 - 7/22/92
90. Teaching Faculty Workload Criteria—8/90
91. Teaching Faculty Workload Criteria—7/92
92. Memorandum to Marion Brady from Robert Aitken re: Grievances, dated April 28, 1992
93. Memorandum to Robert Lawton from Bob Craig re: Marion Brady, dated March 13, 1990
94. Memorandum to Marion Brady from Bob Craig re: LOA, dated March 21, 1990
95. Memorandum to Marion Brady from Bob Craig re: Grievance, dated March 16, 1992
96. Code of Ethics
97. Faculty Schedule, Summer I, 1992—Blackmon
98. Faculty Schedule, Summer I, 1992—Neill
99. Faculty Schedule, Summer, 1992—Johnson
100. Memorandum to Dr. Gene Street from Marion Brady re: Faculty Evaluation, dated January 17, 1984
101. Grievance filed by Marion Brady, dated April 30, 1992
102. Project Abstract
103. Registration Summary, Fall, 1991—J. Brooks
104. Registration Summary, Spring, 1992—J. Brooks
105. Class Roll—J. Brooks
106. Request for Leave of Absence (Composite)
107. Memorandum to Marion Brady from Stevan McCrory re: Grievance dated May 5, 1992, dated May 18, 1992

108. Grievance filed by Marion Brady, dated April 21, 1992 (date of occurrence April 13, 1992)
109. Grievance filed by Marion Brady, dated April 21, 1992 (date of occurrence April 17, 1992)
110. Memorandum to Marion Brady from Stevan McCrory re: Grievance, dated May 12, 1992
111. Grievance filed by Marion Brady, dated May 15, 1992
112. Memorandum to Marion Brady from Stevan McCrory re: Grievance—Date of Occurrence May 18 - June 12, 1992
113. Letter to Maxwell Brady from Maxwell King, dated January 30, 1980
114. Composite exhibit re: 11/18/91 letter of reprimand
     Memorandum to Lawton from McCrory, dated 11/18/91
     Memorandum to Brady from McCrory, dated 11/18/91 re: Letter of Reprimand—Gross Insubordination
     Memorandum to Brady from McCrory, dated 11/18/91 re: Letter of Reprimand—Gross Insubordination with a note at the top "withdrawn by S. McCrory"
     Memorandum to Craig from McCrory, dated 2/3/92 re: Letter of Reprimand
     Memorandum to Lawton from Craig, dated 2/4/92 re: Letters of Reprimand—Marion Brady
     Memorandum to Brady and McCrory from Craig, dated 2/4/92 re: Letters of Reprimand
     Interoffice Memorandum to McCrory from Craig, dated 2/5/92 re: Letter of Reprimand
115. Memorandum to Dr. Bert Purga/Vice President for Academic Affairs/Campus Provosts/Deans from Maxwell C. King, dated 11/15/91 re: Professionalism
116. Memo to Members BCC Board of Trustees from Marion Brady, dated 3/31/92
117. Memorandum to Members, Board of Trustees from Maxwell C. King, dated 4/16/92 (with attachments) re: Marion Brady Letter
118. Letter to Marion Brady from Steve Mittlestet, dated 5/29/92 re: anonymous letter from BCC
119. Composite—Letter to Marion Brady from Robert Lawton, dated 11/15/90 requesting that Marion stay in Dallas for another semester; Letter to Robert Lawton from Joy Brady, dated 11/17/90 stating that Marion will be returning to BCC for the winter term according to his leave of absence
120. Minutes of the Academic Management Team, dated July 22, 1992
121. Administrative Performance Review of Instructional Faculty for Jeffrey W. Reynolds, dated 12/20/91
122. Brooks Syllabus, Philosophy 2010
123. Answer to Interrogatory number 17, signed by Maxwell King on 8/27/92
124. Memorandum to Dr. Maxwell King from Marion Brady, dated 1/17/80
125. Memorandum to Drs. Aitken and Street from Marion Brady, dated 10/25/83 re: College Textbook Policy
126. Memorandum to Dr. Maxwell King from Marion Brady, dated 4/11/88 re: Problems/Solutions
127. Memorandum to Faculty and Staff from Concerned Faculty and Staff, dated 4/18/88 re: Problems
128. Memo to Faculty and Staff from The Green Ribbon Option, dated 4/25/88
129. Memo to Interested Faculty from Marion Brady re: Blue Ribbon Committee
130. Memorandum to Liberal Arts Faculty from Marion Brady, dated 7/14/88 re: Blue Ribbon Committee
131. Letter to Dr. Maxwell King from Marion Brady, dated 9/21/88
132. Statement read by Attorney Kurt Erlenbach at the 2/15/89 meeting of the Board
133. Composite—Marion's evaluations from 1976/77 to 1990
134. Letter to Betty Castor from Val Batts (Concerned Faculty), dated 5/22/89
135. Memorandum to Dr. Maxwell King from Marion Brady, dated 6/5/89
136. *Florida Today* articles

137. Letter to Betty Castor from Marion Brady, dated 9/27/89
138. Memo to Members of the Post-Secondary Education Planning Commission from Marion Brady, dated 12/12/89
139. Guest column by Marion Brady entitled "College needs classrooms, materials instead of festivals and monuments"
140. Letter to John Henry Jones from BCC-UFF Executive Committee: Robert Gregrich, June England, Pat Jones, Connie Bradish, Marion Brady, Neil Hamilton and Jerre Kennedy, dated 4/17/90
141. Speech prepared by Marion Brady, dated 5/30/90
142. Letter to Congressman Bill Nelson from Marion Brady, dated 5/21/90
143. *Florida Today* article by Marion Brady entitled "Agencies scrutinize problems at college," dated 9/4/90
144. Letter to Lawton Chiles from Faculty members, dated 2/11/91
145. Memo to Dr. King from Marion Brady, dated 2/11/91
146. Memo to John Henry J. from Marion B., dated 3/1/91
147. Letter to Marion Brady from John Henry Jones, dated 3/7/91 in response to Marion's recent letter
148. Letter to Senator Arnett Girardeau from UFF-BCC Executive Committee: Marion Brady, Pat Jones, Janis Campbell, Charles Hatfield, Linda Parrish and A. Thornquest, dated 3/4/91
149. Letter to Lawton Chiles from Marion Brady, dated 4/15/91
150. Guest column in *Florida Today* by Marion Brady entitled "If they change college operations, there'll be no more rabble-rousers," dated 11/25/91
151. Letter to Lawton Chiles from Marion Brady, dated 1/9/92
152. Memo to Brevard Community College Trustees from Marion Brady, dated 5/5/92
153. Memo to Brevard Community College Trustees from Marion Brady, dated 5/12/92
154. *Florida Today* article by Marion Brady entitled "What's important are visions of BCC faculty," dated 8/3/92
155. Composite—Student comments from the student evaluations
156. Memo to Stevan McCrory from Marion Brady, dated 11/20/91 re: Charge Against Me of Gross Insubordination
157. Memo to Stevan McCrory from Marion Brady, dated 1/27/92
158. Grievance signed by Marion 3/11/92—annual evaluation for 1991 with 4 "Below Expectations"
159. Interoffice Memorandums (E-mail) from Stevan McCrory, dated 9/26/90, 9/26/90, 10/1/90 and 10/2/90
160. Syllabus for American History—1/92 Term
161. Composite—Reality chart; directions for writing a paper
162. Memo to Robert Aitken from Marion Brady, dated 1/13/92
163. Memorandum to Robert Lawton from Bob Craig, dated 6/16/92 re: Status Report Marion Brady Grievances
164. Memorandum to Liberal Arts/Business Division Faculty from Robert Aitken, dated 5/18/92 re: Summer Term A/92—Discrepancy Rolls
165. Grievance signed by Marion Brady 6/12/92 and received by Robert Aitken—McCrory's observations of Brady's class 4/13/92, 4/15/92 and 4/17/92 and subsequent reprimands
166. Grievance signed by Marion Brady 6/12/92 and received by Robert Aitken—Schedule of classes on Melbourne and Palm Bay campuses
167. Interoffice Memo from Tace Crouse, dated September 25, 1992
168. Deposition transcript of Ann Thomas, dated July 25, 1992
169. Employment Contracts for Marion Brady (Composite)
170. Letter and attachments to Frank Dean, U.S. Department of Labor from Robert Craig re: Payment of Back Wages (Composite)
171. Leave requests and purchase requisitions (Composite)
172. Marion Brady request for transfer memos (Composite)
173. Interoffice Memorandum to Stevan McCrory from Bob Craig re: Brady Grievances on Incomplete forms, dated May 21, 1992

174. Memo to All Concerned Parties from Marion Brady re: Grievances, dated June 15, 1992
175. Memorandum to Marion Brady from Stevan McCrory re: Lost Grievances Submitted to the Provost Office June 15, 1992, dated June 16, 1992
176. Memorandum to Marion Brady from Stevan McCrory re: Grievance— Date of Occurrence May 18 - June 12, 1992, dated June 30, 1992
177. Memorandum to Marion Brady from Robert Aitken re: Grievance— Date of Occurrence: May 18 - June 12, 1992 and May 25, 1992, dated July 15, 1992
178. Response to Grievances to Marion Brady from maxwell King, dated August 6, 1992
179. Memo to Robert Craig from Linda Parrish re: intent to arbitrate Brady grievances, dated August 13, 1992
180. Memorandum to Maxwell King from Bob Craig re: Brady Grievance B-8, dated August 24, 1992
181. Grievance filed by Marion Brady, dated August 21, 1992
182. Grievances filed by Marion Brady, dated September 2, 1992 (Composite)
183. Memorandum to Robert Lawton from Bob Craig re: 3 Grievances, dated September 3, 1992
184. Memorandum to Bert Purga from Marion Brady, dated 6/26/89
185. Note to Ms. Castor (undated)
186. Memo to Brevard Community College Trustees from Marion Brady, dated 5/21/90
187. Letter to Fellow Faculty Member incorporating memo to John Henry Jones from Marion Brady, dated 3/19/91
188. Letter to Linda Rowe from Marion Brady, dated 4/23/91
189. Memo to Dr. Frank Williams from the UFF-BCC Executive Committee, dated 10/23/91
190. Memo to Steve Megregian from Connie Bradish, Marion Brady, Janis Campbell, Robert Gregrich, Pat Jones, Jerre Kennedy, Linda Parrish, Alan Thornquest, Kathy Tickner, dated 10/24/91
191. Memo to Frank Williams from Marion Brady, dated 4/8/92
192. Memo to Brevard Community College Trustees from Marion Brady, dated 6/19/92
193. Guest column by Marion Brady entitled "What is worth teaching? Knowledge explosion is challenging educators"
194. Letter to John Henry Jones from Lewis Nelson, President, ACLU, dated 8/11/92 re: Marion Brady and its objection to the Board hearing the petition to dismiss
195. Letter to John Henry Jones from Concerned Faculty, dated 5/21/92; supportive of Marion
196. Letter to Board of Trustees from Lewis Nelson, President, ACLU, dated 6/10/92
197. Letter to Lewis Nelson from Maxwell King, with attachments, dated 6/11/92
198. Interoffice memorandum to Remote Addressee from Bob Craig, dated 7/9/92 re: Brady retirement risk
199. Memorandum to Marion Brady from Robert Lawton re: Temporary Duty Assignment, dated August 14, 1992
200. Memo to Charles Hatfield from Marion Brady re: Grievances
201. Letter to Frank from Marion Brady, dated May 11, 1990
202. Educational Quality at Brevard Community College
203. Educational Quality at Brevard Community College Part II
204. Letter to the Editor of the *Today* from Marion Brady, dated November 9, 1989
205. Letter to Kenneth Paulson, *Florida Today*, from Marion Brady, dated November 9, 1989
206. On Brevard Community College to *Florida Today*, dated 1989
207. Letter to Robert Kerrigan from Marion Brady, dated August 27, 1990
208. Letter and attachments to Lawton Chiles from Marion Brady, dated October 12, 1990

251. Order in State of Florida vs. Alan Thornquest, Case No. 93-01807-MMA
252. Job Search record of Alan Thornquest
253. Employment Contract for Thomas Ward (Composite)
254. Administrative Performance review of Thomas Ward (Composite)
255. Letter to Thomas Ward from Maxwell King, dated May 2, 1991
256. SACS Faculty Survey Analysis prepared by Thomas Ward
257. Memorandum to Dr. Henry Carrier from Tace Crouse re: Your Memo Dated October 15, 1991, dated October 14, 1991
258. Memorandum to Discipline Coordinator from Henry Carrier, dated October 15, 1991
259. Supplement to Non-Compliance Memorandum Relating to 6.1.0.8., 6.1.0.9., 6.1.0.10., 6.1.1.11. and 6.1.1.12. with handwritten notes
260. Letter to Thomas S. Ward from Robert Lawton, dated March 31, 1992
261. Memorandum to Robert Craig from Thomas Ward re: Request for Academic Due Process Committee hearing, dated April 16, 1992
262. Memorandum to Due Process Committee from Bob Craig re: Due Process Rights, dated May 28, 1992
263. Memorandum and attachments to Dr. Maxwell King through Robert Lawton from Academic Due Process Committee re: Hearing requested by Tom Ward, dated June 10, 1992
264. Interoffice Memorandum to Dr. Maxwell King from Robert Lawton, re: Academic Due Process Committee Findings, dated June 19, 1992
265. Memorandum to Robert Lawton from Maxwell King re: Academic Due Process Committee, dated June 23, 1992
266. Work Search record of Thomas Ward
267. Student Evaluations of Thomas Ward
268. Southern Association of Colleges and Schools Resource Manual On Institutional Effectiveness
269. Southern Association of Colleges and Schools Criteria for Accreditation 1992-1993 edition
270. Brevard Community College Institutional Self-Study Manual 1991-1993
271. Brevard Community College Institutional Self-Study 1991-1993
272. Brevard Community College Institutional Self-Study 1991-1993 Action Plan/Addendum
273. Administrative Performance Review of Julia Brooks
274. All exhibits listed by Defendants
275. Rebuttal exhibits as necessary